Language and Problems of Knowledge

Current Studies in Linguistics Series
Samuel Jay Keyser, general editor

Language and Problems of Knowledge

The Managua Lectures

Noam Chomsky

The MIT Press

Cambridge, Massachusetts

London, England

Ninth printing, 1997

This book was set in Sabon by Achorn Graphic Services and printed
and bound in the United States of America.

Library of Congress Cataloging-in-Publication Data

Chomsky, Noam.
  Language and problems of knowledge.

  (Current studies in linguistics series; 16)
  Includes bibliographical references and index.
  1. Linguistics.   2. Languages—Philosophy.   3. Psycholinguistics.
  4. Knowledge, Theory of.   I. Title.   II. Series.
P125.C47   1988   410   87-3953
ISBN 0-262-03133-7
ISBN 0-262-53070-8 (pbk.)

Contents

Preface

In the first week of March 1986, I had the opportunity to visit Managua and to lecture at the Universidad Centroamericana (UCA), at the invitation of Rector César Jerez, S.J., and also under the auspices of the research center CIDCA, directed by Galio Gurdián. These lectures consisted of a morning series devoted to problems of language and knowledge and a late afternoon series devoted to contemporary political issues. Participants included a wide range of people from the academic community and many others in Nicaragua, as well as visitors from Costa Rican universities and foreigners visiting or working in Nicaragua. The lectures, which I delivered in English, were expertly translated into Spanish for the listening audience by Danilo Salamanca and María-Esther Zamora, who translated the public discussion as well. The proceedings were broadcast (and, I subsequently learned, picked up by short wave in the United States) and transcribed, including the discussions afterward, though inevitably many of the thoughtful and informative comments from the floor were not captured properly on the tape recorder and hence do not appear here.

The chapters that follow consist of somewhat extended versions of the morning lectures on language and knowledge and an edited version of the transcripts of the discussion. The afternoon lectures on contemporary political issues will appear in a separate volume, to be published by South End Press in Boston, with the title *On Power and Ideology: The Managua Lectures*. Because the examples used to illustrate principles of language and to motivate the discussion were in Spanish, I have added some explanation and made a few changes here to facilitate understanding for the English language edition. In attempting to reconstruct the discussion from the transcript, I added material that was missing from the tape in a few places and I have sometimes transferred the discussion from one place to another where it fits more naturally with the edited lectures. I have also eliminated from the discussion a good deal of material that I was able to incorporate into the text of the lectures, essentially in response to queries and interventions by the audience. These interventions thus appear only in fragmentary form, in part because of this editing, in part because of the technical difficulty of recording speakers from the large and diffuse audience in a bilingual discussion, which proceeded with remarkable facility thanks to the translators and good will of the participants. The published transcripts therefore give only a limited indication of the stimulating nature of the comments and questions during the lively and open discussion periods, which were all too short because of the constraints of time.

I would like to express particular thanks to Danilo Salamanca and María-Esther Zamora, not only for the careful way in which they carried out the difficult and trying task of translation in both directions but also for their assistance to me in preparing the lectures. For the Spanish materials that appear in these lectures on linguistics, I am indebted to Esther Torrego for her valuable assistance—the latter term, something of an understatement. I was particularly pleased that Claribel Alegría agreed to undertake the translation of both volumes into

Spanish—both my English text and the discussion transcript—for the Nicaraguan edition.

I would also like to express my thanks—here speaking as well for my wife, Carol, who accompanied me on this visit—to César Jerez, Galio Gurdián, Danilo Salamanca, María-Esther Zamora, Claribel Alegría, and the many others who spent so much time and effort in making our visit a most memorable occasion for us. We much appreciate the gracious hospitality and care of the many friends from many walks of life whom we met in Managua and the opportunity for informative discussions with them and even for some travel and informal visits at their homes, interspersed in a demanding but exhilarating schedule of meetings and lectures. I would also like to thank many people whose names I do not know or remember: the sisters of the Asunción order who welcomed us in the agricultural cooperative they organized in an impoverished peasant community near León, the participants in the public meetings and other discussions, and many others. I might mention particularly the opportunity to meet many people from the wonderful community of exiles from the US-installed horror chambers in the region, who have fled to a place where they can be free from state terror and can live with some dignity and hope—though the Master of the Hemisphere is doing what it can to prevent this grave threat to "order" and "stability."

I expected that Nicaragua would be very different from the picture that filters through the US media, but I was pleased to discover how large the discrepancy is, an experience shared with many other visitors, including people who have lived for extended periods in many parts of the country. It is quite impossible for any honest visitor from the United States to speak about this matter without pain and deep regret, without shame over our inability to bring our fellow citizens to comprehend the meaning and the truth of Simón Bolívar's statement, over 150 years ago, that "the United States seems destined to plague and torment the continent in the name of freedom," over our inability to bring an end to the torture of Nicaragua, and not Nicaragua alone, which our country has taken as its historical vocation for over a century and pursues with renewed dedication today.

A Framework for Discussion

The topics I will address in these five lectures on language and problems of knowledge are intricate and complex and at the same time quite wide ranging in scope. I will try to present some thoughts on these matters in a way that does not require any special knowledge. At the same time I would like to give at least a sense of some of the technical problems that lie near the forefront of research and the kinds of answers that it may be possible today to provide for them, and I want to indicate why I think that these rather technical issues bear on questions of considerable general interest and antiquity.

I will not try to give an exposition of the current state of understanding of language; that would be far too large a task to undertake in the time available. Rather, I will try to present and clarify the kinds of questions with which this study—or at least a major strand within it—is concerned and to place them in a more general context. This context has two aspects: the tradition of Western philosophy and psychology, which have been concerned with understanding the essential nature of human beings; and the attempt within contemporary science to approach traditional questions in the light of what we now know or may hope to learn about organisms and about the brain.

In fact, the study of language is central to both kinds of inquiry: to traditional philosophy and psychology, which constitute a significant part of the history of Western thought, and to contemporary scientific inquiry into human nature. There are several reasons why language has been and will continue to be of particular significance for the study of human nature. One is that language appears to be a true species property, unique to the human species in its essentials and a common part of our shared biological endowment, with little variation among humans apart from rather serious pathology. Furthermore, language enters in a crucial way into thought, action, and social relations. Finally, language is relatively accessible to study. In this respect the topic is quite different from others that we would hope to be able to address: problem solving, artistic creativity, and other aspects of human life and activity.

In discussing the intellectual tradition in which I believe contemporary work finds its natural place, I do not make a sharp distinction between philosophy and science. The distinction, justifiable or not, is a fairly recent one. In dealing with the topics that concern us here, traditional thinkers did not regard themselves as "philosophers" as distinct from "scientists." Descartes, for example, was one of the leading scientists of his day. What we call his "philosophical work" is not separable from his "scientific work" but is rather a component of it concerned with the conceptual foundations of science and the outer reaches of scientific speculation and (in his eyes) inference. David Hume, in his inquiries into human thought, considered his project to be akin to Newton's: He aimed to discover the elements of human nature and the principles that enter into and guide our mental life. The term "philosophy" was used to include what we would call science, so that physics was called natural philosophy and the term "philosophical grammar" meant scientific grammar. Leading figures in the study of language and thought understood philosophical grammar (or general grammar, or universal grammar) to be a deductive science concerned with "the immutable and general principles of spoken or written language," principles that form a part of common human nature and that "are the same as those that direct human reason in its intellectual operations" (Beauzée). Quite commonly, as in this case, the study of language and of thought were regarded as closely related inquiries if not a single endeavor. This particular conclusion, widely expressed in otherwise conflicting traditions, seems to me quite dubious for reasons I discuss in lecture 5; but the general conception of the nature of the inquiry seems sound, and I will keep to it.

A person who speaks a language has developed a certain system of knowledge, represented somehow in the mind and, ultimately, in the brain in some physical configuration. In pursuing an inquiry into these topics, then, we face a series of questions, among them:

1. What is the system of knowledge? What is in the mind/brain of the speaker of English or Spanish or Japanese?

2. How does this system of knowledge arise in the mind/brain?

3. How is this knowledge put to use in speech (or secondary systems such as writing)?

4. What are the physical mechanisms that serve as the material basis for this system of knowledge and for the use of this knowledge?

These are classical questions, though not formulated in quite the terms I will adopt. The first question was the central topic of inquiry in the philosophical grammar of the seventeenth and eighteenth centuries. The second question is a special and important case of what we might *Plato* call Plato's problem. As rephrased by Bertrand Russell in his later work, the problem is basically this: "How comes it that human beings, whose contacts with the world are brief and personal and limited, are able to know as much as they do know?" Plato illustrated the problem with the first recorded psychological experiment (at least, a "thought experiment"). In *The Meno* Socrates demonstrates that an untutored slave boy knows the principles of geometry by leading him, through a series of questions, to the discovery of theorems of geometry. This experiment raises a problem that is still with us: How was the slave boy able to find truths of geometry without instruction or information?

Plato, of course, proposed an answer to this problem: The knowledge was remembered from an earlier existence and was reawakened in the slave boy's mind through the questions that Socrates posed to him. Centuries later, Leibniz argued that Plato's answer was essentially correct but that it must be "purged of the error of preexistence." How can we interpret this proposal in modern terms? A modern variant would be that certain aspects of our knowledge and understanding are innate, part of our biological endowment, genetically determined, on a par with the elements of our common nature that cause us to grow arms and legs rather than wings. This version of the classical doctrine is, I think, essentially correct. It is quite remote from the empiricist assumptions that have dominated much of Western thought for the past several centuries, though not entirely foreign to conceptions of major empiricist thinkers such as Hume, who spoke of those parts of our knowledge that are derived "from the original hand of nature" and that are "a species of instinct."

Plato's problem arises in a striking form in the study of language, and something like the answer just suggested seems to be the right one. I will illustrate as we proceed.

The third question of the series can be divided into two aspects: the perception problem and the production problem. The perception problem has to do with how we interpret what we hear (or read; I put this clearly secondary matter aside here). The production problem, which is considerably more obscure, has to do with what we say and why we say it. We might call this latter problem Descartes's problem. At its heart lies the problem of accounting for what we might call "the creative aspect of language use." Descartes and his followers observed that the normal use of language is constantly innovative, unbounded, apparently free from control by external stimuli or internal states, coherent and appropriate to situations; it evokes thoughts in the listener that he or she might have expressed in similar ways in the same situations. Thus in normal speech one does not merely repeat what one has heard but produces new linguistic forms—often new in one's experience or even in the history of the language—and there are no limits to such innovation. Furthermore, such discourse is not a series of random utterances but fits the situation that evokes it but does not cause it, a crucial if obscure difference. The normal use of language is thus free and undetermined but yet appropriate to situations; and it is recognized as appropriate by other participants in the discourse situation who might have reacted in similar ways and whose thoughts, evoked by this discourse, correspond to those of the speaker. For the Cartesians the creative aspect of language use provided the best evidence that another organism who looks like us has a mind like ours.

The creative aspect of language use was also used as one central argument to establish the conclusion, central to Cartesian thought, that humans are fundamentally different from everything else in the physical world. Other organisms are machines. When their parts are arranged in a certain configuration and they are placed in a certain external environment, then what they do is fully determined (or, perhaps, random). But humans under these conditions are not "compelled" to act in a certain way, but are only "incited and inclined" to do so, as one lead-

ing expositor of Cartesian thought explained. Their behavior may be predictable, in that they will tend to do
what they are incited and inclined to do, but they are
nonetheless free, and uniquely so, in that they need not do
what they are incited and inclined to do. If, for example, I
were to take out a machine gun, point it menacingly at
you, and command you to shout "Heil Hitler," you might
do it if you had reason to believe I was a homicidal ma-
niac, but you would have a choice in the matter, even if
that choice is not exercised. The situation is not unknown
in the real world; under Nazi occupation, for example,
many people—in some countries, the vast majority—
became active or passive collaborators, but some resisted.
A machine, in contrast, acts in accordance with its internal configuration and external environment, with no
choice. The creative aspect of language use was often offered as the most striking example of this fundamental
aspect of human nature.

The fourth question is a relatively new one, in fact
one that is still on the horizon. The first three questions
fall within the domain of linguistics and psychology, two
fields that I would prefer not to distinguish, regarding linguistics (or more precisely, those areas of linguistics with
which I am concerned here) as just that part of psychology that deals with the particular aspects of this discipline
outlined in the first three questions. Let me also stress
again that I would include large areas of philosophy
within the same rubric, following traditional though not
modern practice. Insofar as the linguist can provide answers to questions 1, 2, and 3, the brain scientist can
begin to explore the physical mechanisms that exhibit
the properties revealed in the linguist's abstract theory. In
the absence of answers to these questions, brain scientists
do not know what they are searching for; their inquiry is
in this respect blind.

This is a familiar story in the physical sciences. Thus

nineteenth-century chemistry was concerned with the properties of chemical elements and provided models of compounds (for example, the benzene ring). It developed such notions as valence, molecule, and the periodic table of the elements. All of this proceeded at a level that was highly abstract. How all of this might relate to more fundamental physical mechanisms was unknown, and there was in fact much debate over whether these notions had any "physical reality" or were just convenient myths devised to help organize experience. This abstract inquiry set problems for the physicist: to discover physical mechanisms that exhibit these properties. The remarkable successes of twentieth-century physics have provided increasingly more sophisticated and compelling solutions for these problems in a quest that some feel may be approaching a kind of "ultimate and complete answer."

The study of the mind/brain today can be usefully conceived in much the same terms. When we speak of the mind, we are speaking at some level of abstraction of yet-unknown physical mechanisms of the brain, much as those who spoke of the valence of oxygen or the benzene ring were speaking at some level of abstraction about physical mechanisms, then unknown. Just as the discoveries of the chemist set the stage for further inquiry into underlying mechanisms, so today the discoveries of the linguist-psychologist set the stage for further inquiry into brain mechanisms, inquiry that must proceed blindly, without knowing what it is looking for, in the absence of such understanding, expressed at an abstract level.

We may ask whether the linguist's constructions are correct or whether they should be modified or replaced. But there are few meaningful questions about the "reality" of these constructions—their "psychological reality," to use the common but highly misleading term—just as there are few meaningful questions about the "physical reality" of the chemist's constructions, though it is always possible to question their accuracy. At every stage of inquiry we try to construct theories that enable us to gain insight into the nature of the world, focusing our attention on those phenomena of the world that provide enlightening evidence for these theoretical endeavors. In the study of language we proceed abstractly, at the level of mind, and we also hope to be able to gain understanding of how the entities constructed at this abstract level and their properties and the principles that govern them can be accounted for in terms of properties of the brain. If the brain sciences succeed in discovering these properties of the brain, we will not cease to discuss language in terms of words and sentences, nouns and verbs, and other abstract concepts of linguistics, just as the chemist today does not refrain from speaking about valence, elements, benzene rings, and the like. These may well remain the appropriate concepts for explanation and prediction, now fortified by an understanding of their relation to more fundamental physical entities—or further inquiry may show that they should be replaced by other abstract conceptions, better suited to the task of explanation and prediction.

Notice that there is nothing mystical about the study of mind, regarded as a study of the abstract properties of brain mechanisms. Rather, contemporary mentalism, so conceived, is a step toward assimilating psychology and linguistics within the physical sciences. Later, I want to return to this topic, which I think is often misunderstood in social science and philosophy, including the Marxist tradition.

I take the four questions as the essential framework for further inquiry. I have nothing to say about question 4 because little is known. I also address question 3 only in part; in its production aspect, at least, question 3 seems to raise problems of a rather different nature, to which I will turn later, but suggesting nothing substantive. With regard to questions 1 and 2 and the perception aspect of 3, there is a good deal to say. Here, there has really been substantial progress.

Questions 1 and 3—the question of what constitutes knowledge of language and how this knowledge is used—are often assimilated. Thus it is often held that to speak and understand a language is to have a practical ability, rather like the ability to ride a bicycle or play chess. More generally, to have knowledge, in this view, is to have certain abilities and skills. It is often argued further that abilities and skills reduce to habits and dispositions, so that language is a habit system, or a system of dispositions to behave in a certain way under certain conditions. The problem of the creative aspect of language use, if noticed at all (it rarely has been until quite recently, after a lapse of a century or more), is explained away in terms of "analogy": Speakers produce new forms "on the analogy" of those they have heard and understand new forms in the same way. Following this line of thought, we avoid the fear of "mentalism," of something occult. We exorcise the Cartesian "ghost in the machine," so it is argued.

The latter qualms are misconceived, as I have mentioned, and I believe they also reflect a serious misunderstanding of traditional mentalism, a matter to which I return in the last lecture. But the idea that knowledge is ability is also entirely untenable. Simple considerations show that this conception can hardly be correct.

Consider two people who share exactly the same knowledge of Spanish: Their pronunciation, knowledge of the meaning of words, grasp of sentence structure, and so on, are identical. Nevertheless, these two people may—and characteristically do—differ greatly in their ability to use the language. One may be a great poet, the second an utterly pedestrian language user who speaks in clichés. Characteristically, two people who share the same knowledge will be inclined to say quite different things on given occasions. Hence it is hard to see how knowledge can be identified with ability, still less with disposition to behavior.

Furthermore, ability can improve with no change in knowledge. A person may take a course in public speaking or composition, thereby improving his or her ability to use the language but gaining no new knowledge of the language: The person has the same knowledge of the words, the constructions, the rules, etc., as before. The ability to use the language has improved, but the knowledge has not. Similarly, ability can be impaired or can disappear with no loss of knowledge. Suppose that Juan, a speaker of Spanish, suffers aphasia after a severe head wound, losing all ability to speak and understand. Has Juan lost his knowledge of Spanish? Not necessarily, as we might discover if Juan recovers his ability to speak and understand as the effects of the injury recede. Of course, Juan recovers the ability to speak and understand *Spanish,* not Japanese, and does so even without any instruction or relevant experience with Spanish. Had his native language been Japanese, he would have recovered the ability to speak and understand *Japanese,* not Spanish, also without instruction or experience. If Juan had lost knowledge of Spanish when he lost the ability to speak and understand Spanish, the recovery of this ability would be a miracle. Why did Juan come to speak Spanish and not Japanese? How did he develop this ability without instruction or experience, something that no child can do? Plainly something was retained while the ability to speak and to understand was lost. What was retained was not the ability, because that was lost. What was retained was a system of knowledge, a *cognitive system* of the mind/ brain. Evidently, possession of this knowledge cannot be identified with ability to speak and understand or with a system of dispositions, skills, or habits. We cannot exorcise the "ghost in the machine" by reducing knowledge to ability, behavior, and dispositions.

Similar considerations show that knowing how to ride a bicycle or how to play chess, and so on, cannot be reduced to systems of abilities and dispositions. Suppose that Juan knows how to ride a bicycle, then suffers a brain injury that causes him to lose this ability completely (while leaving his physical capacities otherwise fully intact), then recovers the ability as the effects of the injury recede. Again something remained unaffected by the injury that caused a temporary loss of ability. What remained intact was the cognitive system that constitutes knowing how to ride a bicycle; this is not simply a matter of ability, disposition, habit, or skill.

To avoid these conclusions, philosophers committed to the identification of knowledge and ability have been forced to conclude that Juan, who lost the ability to speak and understand Spanish after brain injury, in fact retained this ability, though he lost the ability to exercise it.[1] We now have two concepts of ability, one referring to the ability that was retained and the other to the ability that was lost. The two concepts, however, are quite different. It is the second that corresponds to ability in the sense of normal usage; the first is just a new invented concept, designed to have all the properties of knowledge. Not surprisingly, we can now conclude that knowledge is ability, in this new invented sense of "ability" that is quite unrelated to its normal sense. Plainly nothing is achieved by these verbal maneuvers. We must conclude, rather, that

---

1. For the most detailed recent exposition of this view, see Anthony Kenny, *The Legacy of Wittgenstein* (Oxford: Blackwell, 1984). For more detailed discussion, including remarks on Kenny's critique of my own views on the topic, see my article "Language and Problems of Knowledge," forthcoming in *Teorema* (Madrid).

the attempt to account for knowledge in terms of ability (disposition, skill, etc.) is misconceived from that start. This is one of several respects in which the conception of knowledge that has been developed in much of contemporary philosophy seems to me quite wide of the mark.

Other considerations lead to the same conclusion. Thus Juan knows that the phrase *el libro* refers to a book, not to a table. This is not a failure of ability on his part. It is not because he is too weak, or lacks some skill, that *el libro* fails to refer to tables for Juan. Rather, this is a property of a certain system of knowledge that he possesses. To speak and understand Spanish is to possess such knowledge.

Let us turn to some harder and more interesting examples that illustrate the same points and that will lead us to a clearer understanding of Plato's problem and the challenges it poses. Consider the following sentences:[2]

(1)
Juan arregla el carro.
"Juan fixes the car."

(2)
Juan afeita a Pedro.
Juan shaves to Pedro.
"Juan shaves Pedro."

These sentences illustrate a certain feature of Spanish not shared with such similar languages as Italian: When the object of the verb is animate, as in (2), the object (here, *Pedro*) must be preceded by the preposition *a* ("to") in Spanish, though not in Italian.

Let us now consider another construction of Spanish

---

2. Here and throughout this book Spanish examples are given with a word-by-word English translation below, along with a paraphrase in quotes, unless the word-by-word translation is identical with the paraphrase, as in the case of (1).

in which the verbs *arreglar* ("fix") and *afeitar* ("shave") can appear, the causative construction:

(3)
Juan hizo [arreglar el carro].
Juan made [fix the car].
"Juan had someone fix the car."

(4)
Juan hizo [afeitar a Pedro].
Juan made [shave to Pedro].
"Juan had someone shave Pedro."

The brackets enclose a clausal element that is the *complement* of the verb *hacer* ("make," "cause"): The meaning is that Juan caused a certain event, expressed by the proposition in brackets, namely, that someone fix the car (in (3)) or that someone shave Pedro (in (4)). In (4), the animate object, *Pedro,* once again requires the preposition *a.*

In these examples the subject of the complement clause is unexpressed and is therefore interpreted as someone unspecified. But it might be explicitly expressed:

(5)
Juan hizo [arreglar el carro a María].
Juan made [fix the car to Maria].
"Juan had Maria fix the car."

Here we observe a difference between English and Spanish. In Spanish, the subject of the embedded complement clause appears in an adjoined prepositional phrase (*a María*), whereas in the corresponding English sentence it appears in the normal preverbal position, as in "Maria fixed the car." We return to the reasons for these differences. In this case Spanish behaves just like closely related languages such as Italian.

Suppose now that we attempt to construct an analogue to (5), using the phrase *afeitar a Pedro* instead of *arreglar el carro.* Thus we have the form:

(6)

Juan hizo [afeitar a Pedro a María].
Juan made [shave to Pedro to Maria].
"Juan had Maria shave Pedro."

Sentence (6), however, is unacceptable, though its analogue in Italian would be fine. The reason is that the repetition of two such a-phrases is not permitted, in Spanish as in related languages.[3] Since the object of "shave" in Italian does not require the preposition a, the Italian analogue of (6) is a perfectly acceptable sentence.

In these examples we see illustrated rules of language of varying degrees of generality. At the most general level, in English, Italian, and Spanish it is possible to form causative constructions by embedding a clause as complement to the causative verb; in fact, this is a general property of language, though the precise realization of such abstract forms varies from language to language. At a lower level of generality, English differs from Spanish and Italian in that the subject of the embedded clause remains in its normal subject position in English, whereas it becomes a prepositional a-phrase (or may remain unexpressed) in Italian and Spanish. This distinction, as we will see, follows from deeper distinctions between English on the one hand and Spanish and Italian on the other; for the moment let us simply give the name "the embedded clause property" to these deeper distinctions, whatever they turn out to be. English interprets the embedded clause property differently from Spanish and Italian. This difference entails various consequences, as in the case of causative constructions just illustrated. At a still finer level of detail,

---

3. The story is more complex. Thus if one of the a-phrases is a true prepositional phrase, as in *Juan tiró a su amigo al agua* ("Juan threw his friend into the water"), then the construction is acceptable. But where both occurrences of a are inserted for syntactic reasons and are semantically empty, the construction is barred. I overlook this and further complexities here.

Spanish differs from Italian in that an animate object must be preceded by the preposition *a*, though they share the more general principle that bars the successive *a*-phrases, a principle that entails that (6) is unacceptable in Spanish.

Summarizing, we have general principles, such as the principle for forming causative and other embedded constructions and the principle barring successive *a*-phrases; principles that admit some variation in interpretation, such as the embedded clause property; and low-level rules differentiating very similar languages, such as the rule that requires insertion of *a* in Spanish before an animate object. Of course, these levels are not exhaustive. The interaction of such rules and principles determines the form and interpretation of the expressions of the language.

Let us now reconsider these facts from the point of view of the child learning Spanish. Notice that every example cited poses an instance of Plato's problem. We must determine how the child comes to master the rules and principles that constitute the mature system of knowledge of language. The problem is an empirical one. In principle, the source of such knowledge might lie in the child's environment or in the biologically determined resources of the mind/brain, specifically, that component of the mind/brain that we may call the language faculty; interaction of these factors provides the system of knowledge that is put to use in speaking and understanding. Insofar as knowledge is based on environmental factors, it must be that the mind/brain provides a way to identify and extract the relevant information by means of mechanisms of some sort that are part of its biologically determined resources. Such mechanisms might be specific to the language faculty, or they might be more general "learning mechanisms." Thus, in principle, we have three factors to consider: the genetically determined principles of the language faculty, the genetically determined general learning mechanisms, and the linguistic experience of the child growing up in a speech community. The problem is to sort out and identify these factors. Of these factors we are certain about the existence of the third (simply because of the existence of different languages), and we have quite strong evidence for the existence of the first (principles of the language faculty). The status of general learning mechanisms is far less clear, contrary to what is widely assumed.

In connection with the examples just discussed, we can begin with some plausible speculations. A low-level rule such as the rule of *a*-insertion before animate objects is an idiosyncratic property of Spanish, which must be learned by the child acquiring Spanish; thus the linguistic environment must play some role in this case, interacting either with principles of the language faculty or with some general learning mechanism (if such general mechanisms exist). But the Spanish-speaking child does not have to learn that (6) is an unacceptable sentence; this fact follows from the general principle that bars the successive *a*-phrases. The latter principle might be an element of the language faculty itself, hence available independent of experience, or it might arise from some interaction of experience and innate mechanisms of the language faculty or of learning. As for the embedded clause property, at least some feature of it is determined by the linguistic environment, since languages differ with regard to this property, as we have seen. To introduce some terminology that I will use later on, the embedded clause property is associated with a *parameter; it is parametrized.* This parameter may have one or another *value,* though the general form of the principle is invariant apart from this parametric variation. The value of the parameter must be determined from experience. Once the value is learned, a variety of facts follow by general principles of language, such as those phenomena just illustrated.

Turning to still more general principles, it is reasonable to speculate that the possibility of forming complex constructions with an embedded clausal complement involves no learning at all. Rather, this possibility is simply available as a principle of the language faculty, though the realizations of such abstract constructions will differ depending on lexical and other properties specific to various languages.

Returning to Plato's problem in the light of these remarks, the problem is solved in terms of certain properties of the mind/brain and certain features of the linguistic environment. The properties of the mind/brain include several principles of the language faculty: the availability of complex constructions with an embedded clausal complement, the embedded clause property with its open parameter, perhaps the barrier against the successive *a*-phrases. The linguistic environment must be rich enough to determine the value of the parameter associated with the embedded clause property and to determine that animate objects require *a*-insertion in Spanish. There may or may not be general learning mechanisms involved in these processes. The interaction of these factors produces a system of knowledge that is represented in the mind/brain, as the mature state of the language faculty. This system of knowledge provides the interpretation of linguistic expressions, including new ones that the child learning the language has never heard. Of course, this sketch touches on only a few of the elements involved while illustrating their general character. This is the path we must follow if we hope to solve Plato's problem.

Let us consider now some further complications. In place of *a Pedro* in (2), we might have a reflexive element, referring back to Juan. Spanish permits two possibilities for choice of reflexive: *se* or *sí mismo*. Let us consider here just the first of these. Replacing *Pedro* by *se*, we derive:

(7)

Juan afeita a se.

Juan shaves to himself.

But (7) is not a proper sentence. Rather, the element *se* is what is called technically a clitic, a form that cannot stand alone but must attach to some verb. There is a rule of Spanish, then, that moves *se* from the normal position of direct object of *afeitar,* attaching it to the verb, yielding in the present case[4]

(8)

Juan se afeita.

Juan self-shaves.

"Juan shaves himself."

The reflexive form corresponding to (2), then, is (8). Comparable facts hold for Italian and other languages that have clitic pronouns, including reflexives.

Suppose now that we combine the causative and reflexive constructions, replacing *Pedro* in (4) by the clitic *se,* yielding

(9)

Juan hizo [afeitar a se].

Juan made [shave to self].

Since *se* is a clitic that cannot stand alone, it must move to attach to a verb. Here there are two theoretical possibilities: The clitic may attach to *afeitar,* yielding (10a), or to *hizo,* yielding (10b), where it precedes the verb as in the simple form (8):

---

4. The reflexive pronoun *se* is third person but neutral with regard to gender and number; thus it corresponds to "himself," "herself," "themselves." I translate it as "self," though "3-self" would be more precise.

(10)

a. Juan hizo [afeitarse].
Juan made [shave-self].

b. Juan se hizo [afeitar].
Juan self-made [shave].
"Juan had someone shave him (Juan)."

The second form, (10b), is the normal one for all Spanish dialects (and other related languages, such as Italian). The status of the first one, (10a), is more complex. This construction seems to be unacceptable to speakers of Latin American Spanish and to many speakers in the Spanish of the Iberian Peninsula. Nevertheless, the construction seems acceptable for some variants of Peninsular Spanish. We thus have still another feature that is not a general property of language but rather an idiosyncratic property of particular languages, which must be learned: The rule that attaches a clitic to a verb has a parameter that admits two values, distinguishing (10a) from (10b); or, more likely, this distinction follows from other properties of the languages in question, at least in part learned. In (10b) it is clear that the reflexive *se* refers to Juan. In (10a) the situation is a bit more complex. I put this case to the side for the moment, concentrating now on (10b).

In sentence (10b) the embedded complement of the causative verb is subjectless, as in (3) and (4). But as we have seen, the subject of the complement can be explicit, appearing as an *a*-phrase. If the subject of the complement is, say, *los muchachos* ("the boys"), then we should expect to find

(11)
Juan se hizo [afeitar a los muchachos].
Juan self-made [shave to the boys].
"Juan had the boys shave him (Juan)."

But now a problem arises. Although (10b) is a fine sentence, the result of adding *a los muchachos* to it yields a form with no interpretation: Sentence (11) is not a normal sentence meaning that Juan had the boys shave Juan, analogous to (10b), which means that Juan had someone whose identity is unspecified shave Juan. Somehow the analogy fails. In this case we cannot appeal to the barrier against repeated *a*-phrases to explain why (11) is unacceptable, because there is no repeated *a*-phrase. Rather, some other principle is involved. And indeed we find that in Italian too the analogue to (11) is unacceptable, as a consequence of this other principle.

We see, then, that adding the phrase *a los muchachos* to the causative-reflexive construction changes its status quite considerably, leading to the breakdown of the natural analogies. The same is true if we add the phrase *a quién* to the beginning of this construction. Adding this phrase to (10b) we derive (12), with a change of word order induced by the question phrase *a quién:*

(12)
A quién se hizo Juan [afeitar]?
To whom self-made Juan [shave]?

The sentence again is completely unacceptable in Spanish and Italian, just as (11) is: It does not mean "Whom did Juan have [shave him (Juan)]," as we would expect from the analogous forms. Addition of the phrase *a quién* changes the status of the construction and breaks down natural analogies.

These examples again give rise to Plato's problem, now in a still sharper and more serious form: How does the child learning Spanish and Italian know such facts as these? The examples also reveal once again the hopelessness of an attempt to account for knowledge in terms of ability or to account for the use of language in terms of analogy.

The facts just reviewed form part of the knowledge of speakers of Spanish. The question, then, is how speakers of Spanish come to know these facts. Surely it is not the result of some specific course of training or instruction; nothing of the sort occurs in the course of normal language acquisition. Nor does the child erroneously produce or interpret the sentences (11) or (12) "by analogy" to (10b) and (5), leading to correction of this error by the parent or other teacher; it is doubtful that anyone has undergone this experience and it is certain that not everyone who knows the facts has done so. Furthermore, whatever the resulting knowledge is, it certainly is not identifiable with some kind of ability or skill. Just as speakers of Spanish do not fail to interpret *el libro* as referring to tables because of some lack of skill or ability, so they do not fail to interpret *Juan se hizo afeitar a los muchachos* (with an *a*-phrase subject in the embedded clause) or *A quién se hizo Juan afeitar* "by analogy" to *Juan se hizo afeitar* because of some lack of skill or ability, which they could overcome by more training or practice. Rather, the system of knowledge that has developed in the mind/brain of the speaker of Spanish simply assigns no interpretation to these sentences.

Perhaps the speaker of Spanish, forced to assign some interpretation to these unacceptable sentences, would do so, possibly by analogy to *Juan se hizo afeitar.* This would be a genuine case of use of analogy; normal use of language, however, is not.

Let us return now to the example (10a), repeated here, in which the clitic *se* has attached to the verb *afeitar:*

(10a)
Juan hizo [afeitarse].
Juan made [shave-self].

For Spanish dialects that accept this construction, *se* may be understood (possibly with some awkwardness) to refer to the unexpressed subject of *afeitar,* some unspecified person *x*, so that the sentence would mean that Juan had *x* shave himself (namely, *x*), whoever *x* may be. Suppose, however, that we were to add the phrase *por el barbero* to (10a), yielding

(13)
Juan hizo [afeitarse por el barbero].
Juan made [shave-self by the barber].
"Juan had the barber shave him (Juan)."

Here *se* refers to Juan, so that the sentence means that Juan caused that the barber shave Juan. As to the choice between (13) and the alternative (14), the latter appears to be the standard form:

(14)
Juan se hizo [afeitar por el barbero].
Juan self-made [shave by the barber].
"Juan had the barber shave him (Juan)."

To summarize, for the causative of the reflexive in the full range of dialects we are considering, we have the forms (15a)–(15c) in which *se* refers to Juan, and (15d), in which it refers to some unspecified person, with dialect variation in the case of (15c) and (15d):

(15)
a. Juan se hizo [afeitar por el barbero].
   Juan self-made [shave by the barber].
   "Juan had the barber shave him (Juan)."
b. Juan se hizo [afeitar].
   Juan self-made [shave].
   "Juan had someone shave him (Juan)."
c. Juan hizo [afeitarse por el barbero].
   Juan made [shave-self by the barber].
   "Juan had the barber shave him (Juan)."

d. Juan hizo [afeitarse].
Juan made [shave-self].
"Juan had someone shave (that is, shave himself, not Juan)."

    Suppose now that we add *a los muchachos* to (10a) deriving

(16)
Juan hizo [afeitarse a los muchachos].
Juan made [shave-self to the boys].
"Juan had the boys shave (themselves)."

Here the meaning is plain for those who accept the construction. It means that Juan caused that each of the boys shave himself; *se* refers to the boys, not to Juan. Thus (16) is not interpreted on the analogy of (13), in which *se* refers to Juan:

(13)
Juan hizo [afeitarse por el barbero].

    Suppose that we add *a quién* to (10a), yielding

(17)
A quién hizo Juan [afeitarse]?
To whom made Juan [shave-self]?
"Who did Juan have shave (himself, not Juan)?"

As in the case of (16), here also *se* does not refer to Juan on the analogy of (13); sentence (17) does not ask who is the person who Juan caused to shave Juan. Rather, it asks who is the person who Juan caused to shave that person. The answer could be *a Pedro,* meaning that Juan had Pedro shave Pedro himself, not Juan.

    Again, the speakers of these dialects of Spanish (essentially, different but very similar languages) know these facts without instruction or experience. To the extent that dialects differ, there must be possibilities of variation permitted by the fixed biological endowment, these possibilities being resolved by experience; the same must be true of the variety of languages more generally. But a great deal is constant, determined quite independently of experience. Analogy seems to be a useless concept, invoked simply as an expression of ignorance as to what the operative principles and processes really are. I will return to the operative principles in these more complex cases. For the moment it suffices to recognize that a serious and rather mysterious problem arises in such cases as these, since evidently the speakers of Spanish have a rich system of knowledge, with complex and curious consequences, a system that extends far beyond any specific instruction or experience more generally.

We conclude, again, that a system of knowledge develops in the mind/brain, giving rise to Plato's problem, here illustrated with quite simple and short sentences; the problem, already difficult enough, rapidly becomes far more serious as we consider less simple cases. We also see that knowledge is not ability, that it is not explicable in terms of skills, habits, or dispositions, and that Descartes's problem, or other problems concerning use of language, is not clarified by resort to the vague concept of "analogy."

It should be emphasized once again that the facts just reviewed are known to speakers of Spanish without instruction. Children do not receive relevant instruction or experience about these matters; nor are they typically (or ever) corrected for errors in such cases as these. They do not, for example, interpret *Juan se hizo afeitar a los muchachos* or *A quién se hizo Juan afeitar?* on the analogy of *Juan se hizo afeitar* and then hear from their parents or teachers that for some reason the sentence is not well formed when *a los muchachos* or *a quién* is added. Examples of this kind are not even discussed in grammar books or in instructional manuals for the teaching of Spanish to foreigners. We cannot assume that the sen-

25 tences with *a los muchachos* or *a quién* are rejected because the child has not heard them; normal discourse regularly consists of novel utterances, and in fact people generally do not have the slightest idea whether they have heard a particular sentence or not. Surely few if any readers have come across the sentence they are now reading, and someone who had by chance heard or seen it could not possibly remember such a fact. Hence there is no reason on these grounds why the child learning Spanish should not interpret the sentences with *a los muchachos* or *a quién* "on the analogy" of simpler ones.

The facts reviewed are simply part of the knowledge that grows in the mind/brain of the child exposed to the use of Spanish. They are known because that is the way the human mind works. The properties of these expressions reflect principles of mental operation that form part of the human language faculty. There is no further reason why the facts are the way they are.

These illustrations of Plato's problem were simple ones, but they were drawn from the richest and most complex area of language structure: the constructions and principles that enter into determining the form and the interpretation of sentences. But the problems arise elsewhere as well and are no less serious.

Take the question of sound structure. Here too the person who has acquired knowledge of a language has quite specific knowledge about facts that transcend his or her experience, for example, about which nonexistent forms are possible words and which are not. Consider the forms *strid* and *bnid*. Speakers of English have not heard either of these forms, but they know that *strid* is a possible word, perhaps the name of some exotic fruit they have not seen before, but *bnid*, though pronounceable, is not a possible word of the language. Speakers of Arabic, in contrast, know that *bnid* is a possible word and *strid* is not; speakers of Spanish know that neither *strid* nor *bnid* is a possible word of their language. The facts can be explained in terms of rules of sound structure that the language learner comes to know in the course of acquiring the language.

Acquisition of the rules of sound structure, in turn, depends on fixed principles governing possible sound systems for human languages, the elements of which they are constituted, the manner of their combination and the modifications that they may undergo in various contexts. These principles are common to English, Arabic, Spanish, and all other human languages and are used unconsciously by a person acquiring any of these languages; the principles belong to the innate language faculty, a component of the mind/brain. These principles of the language faculty, again, are not logically necessary. We can easily construct systems that would violate them, but these would not be human languages. They could perhaps be learned, but by other faculties of the mind, not the language faculty. An arduous course of explicit instruction or training might well be necessary to teach them, or they would have to be discovered as we discover principles of chemistry or physics; or as we discover the principles that enter into human language when we approach the problem as scientists attempting to develop conscious knowledge and understanding of facts about the world, not as language learners making use of principles incorporated in our mind/brain but without awareness and beyond any possibility of introspection.

Suppose one were to argue that the knowledge of possible words is derived "by analogy." The explanation is empty until an account is given of this notion. If we attempt to develop a concept of "analogy" that will account for these facts, we will discover that we are building into this notion the rules and principles of sound structure. There is no general notion of "analogy" that applies to these and other cases. Rather, the term is being used, in an extremely misleading way, to refer to the properties of particular subsystems of our knowledge, entirely different properties in different cases.

The solution to Plato's problem must be based on ascribing the fixed principles of the language faculty to the human organism as part of its biological endowment. These principles reflect the way the mind works, within the language faculty.

A striking fact about language acquisition in the young child is the degree of precision with which the child imitates the speech of its models (family members, other children, or whatever). The precision of phonetic detail goes far beyond what adults can perceive without special training and thus cannot possibly be the result of any form of training (quite apart from this, language acquisition commonly proceeds on course even without any concern on the part of the models and probably quite independently of such concern, if it is manifested, with marginal exceptions). The child is evidently hearing—not consciously, of course—details of phonetic nuance that it will incorporate as part of its linguistic knowledge but that in adult life it will no longer be able to detect.

Similar problems arise in the area of vocabulary acquisition, and the solution to them must lie along the same lines: in the biological endowment that constitutes the human language faculty. At the peak period of vocabulary growth, the child masters words at quite an astonishing rate, perhaps a dozen a day or more. Anyone who has attempted to define a word precisely knows that this is an extremely difficult matter, involving intricate and complex properties. Ordinary definitions in monolingual or bilingual dictionaries do not even come close to characterizing the meaning of the word, nor need they do so, because the dictionary maker can assume that the user of the dictionary already possesses the linguistic competence incorporated within the language faculty of the mind/

brain. The speed and precision of vocabulary acquisition leaves no real alternative to the conclusion that the child somehow has the concepts available before experience with language and is basically learning labels for concepts that are already part of his or her conceptual apparatus. This is why dictionary definitions can be sufficient for their purpose, though they are so imprecise. The rough approximation suffices because the basic principles of word meaning (whatever they are) are known to the dictionary user, as they are to the language learner, independently of any instruction or experience.

These principles of word meaning are quite subtle and surprising. Consider a simple word such as *libro*. Without instruction or relevant experience, each speaker of Spanish knows that this word can receive either an abstract or a concrete interpretation. In sentence (18), for example, the word is interpreted concretely, referring to some specific physical object, whereas in (19) it is interpreted abstractly, referring to some abstract entity that may have a wide range of physical instantiations (though not without limits):

(18)
El libro pesa dos kilos.
"The book weighs two kilos."

(19)
Juan escribió un libro.
"Juan wrote a book."

Furthermore, the word can be used with both meanings simultaneously, as in

(20)
Juan escribió un libro de política, que pesa dos kilos.
"Juan wrote a book about politics that weighs two kilos."

Here, the phrase *libro de política* is used in its abstract sense as the object of the verb *escribir* ("write") in the main clause but in its concrete sense as the subject of the verb *pesar* ("weigh") in the relative clause. The sentence has roughly the meaning of the conjunction of the two sentences of (21):

(21)
Juan escribió un libro de política; el libro pesa dos kilos.
"Juan wrote a book about politics; the book weighs two kilos."

The abstract sense of *un libro de política* in the main clause is brought out more clearly in such sentences as (22):

(22)
Juan escribió un libro de política, que pesa dos kilos en tela y un kilo en rústica.
"Juan wrote a book about politics, which weighs two kilos in hardcover and one kilo in paperback."

Here *un libro de política* refers to an abstract entity, which can be instantiated in different ways.

The situation is naturally quite different in other cases when a word has two meanings. Take the word *gata* in colloquial Spanish; it can refer to a female cat or to a device for lifting a car (in other dialects, *gato*). But sentence (23) does not have the meaning (24), analogous to (21):

(23)
Juan tiene una gata que puede levantar el carro.
Juan has a cat/jack that can lift the car.

(24)
Juan tiene una gata; la gata puede levantar el carro.
"Juan has a cat/jack; the cat/jack can lift the car."

The relationship that holds between the word in the main clause and its unexpressed duplicate in the relative clause in (23) does not suffice to yield the interpretation of (24), though the relationship does suffice for (20) and (22). The same phenomena can be illustrated in English. Thus the word *book* has the properties of (18)–(20), as illustrated, but a word such as *trunk* (long snout of an elephant, large luggage container) does not; sentence (25a) does not have the meaning of (25b), and in (26) we understand the phrase *elephant's trunk* to refer to the elephant's luggage container:

(25)
a. The elephant has a trunk, which is packed full of clothes.
b. The elephant has a trunk (long snout); the trunk (luggage container) is packed full of clothes.

(26)
I gazed at the elephant's trunk, which was packed full of clothes.

Such phenomena are obvious to speakers of any language. The facts are known without relevant experience, and they need not be taught to a person learning Spanish or English as a second language. Spelling out exactly what is involved and how broadly the relevant principles apply is not a simple matter, and in fact it has never been done except casually and imprecisely. Evidently, the facts come to be known on the basis of a biological endowment that is prior to any experience and that enters into determining the meaning of words with remarkable precision and surely not in any way that is logically necessary. A possible language could function in quite a different way, but it would not be a human language and could be learned by humans only with difficulty, if at all.

The same is true with regard to the simplest concepts, for example, the concept of a nameable thing, which turns out to have remarkable intricacies, even involving the sophisticated idea of human agency, when one investigates it closely. Similarly the concept of a person, one of the most primitive concepts available to a young child, is extremely complex and has been the subject of subtle philosophical inquiry for many centuries. Surely none of this is learned through experience. In fact, to explore the bounds of the concepts that we possess and use without thought or awareness, we must construct invented examples, and this is far from a simple task.

The concepts that are available, independently of experience, to be associated with (or labeled by) words in a human language do not constitute a mere list. Rather, like the sounds of language, they enter into systematic structures based on certain elementary recurrent notions and principles of combination. Ideas such as action, agent of an action, goal, intent, and others, enter into the concepts of thought and language in complex ways. Consider the words *seguir* ("follow") and *perseguir* ("chase"). The latter involves human intention. To chase someone is not merely to follow him; in fact, one may chase someone without exactly following his path, and one may be following someone's path precisely at a fixed distance from him without chasing him (by accident, for example). Rather, to chase someone is to follow him (in some rather loose sense) with a certain intention: the intention to keep on his trail and perhaps (but not necessarily) to catch him. Similarly, the word *persuadir* ("persuade") involves the notion of causation as well as the notion of intention or decision (along with much else). To persuade John to go to college is to cause John to decide or intend to go to college; if John at no point decides or intends to go to college, then I have not persuaded him to go to college, however much I may have tried. The situation is in fact a good bit more complex. I may cause John to decide to go to college by force or threat, but without having persuaded him to go to college, strictly speaking. Persuasion involves volition. If I say that the police interrogator persuaded John to confess by the threat of torture, I am using the term "persuade" ironically. Someone who knows no Spanish at all will know these facts about the word *persuadir,* and the same is true, in essence, of the child learning Spanish—or English or other human languages. The child must have enough information to determine that the form *persuadir* is the one that corresponds to the preexisting concept but need not discover the precise bounds and intricacies of this concept, which is already available, before experience with language.

The child approaches language with an intuitive understanding of such concepts as physical object, human intention, volition, causation, goal, and so on. These constitute a framework for thought and language and are common to the languages of the world, though even languages so similar in character and in the cultural background of their use as English and Spanish may differ somewhat in the means of expression used, as a speaker of one quickly discovers when trying to learn the other. For example, the English word corresponding to the Spanish *persuadir* is *persuade,* in one of its senses a causative based on the concept expressed in English by the single word *intend* but in Spanish by the phrase *tener intención.* Nevertheless, though words may not match precisely across languages, the conceptual framework in which they find their place is a common human property. The extent to which this framework can be modified by experience and varying cultural contexts is a matter of debate, but it is beyond question that acquisition of vocabulary is guided by a rich and invariant conceptual system, which is prior to any experience. The same is true even for the technical concepts of the natural sciences, which the scientist acquires on the basis of only partial information and evidence, a good deal simply being taken for granted, without explicit or precise expression, except at the higher reaches of the sophisticated mathematical sciences.

One conclusion that seems quite well established on the basis of considerations such as these is that some statements are known to be true independently of any experience. They are what are called truths of meaning, not truths of empirical fact. Without knowing anything about the facts of the matter, I know that if you persuaded John to go to college, then at some point he intended or decided to go to college; if he did not, then you did not persuade him. The statement that to persuade John to do something is to cause him to intend or decide to do that thing is necessarily true. It is true by virtue of the meaning of its terms, independently of any facts; it is an "analytic truth" in technical jargon. On the other hand, to know whether the statement that John went to college is true, I must know certain facts about the world.

One of the widely accepted and quite influential conclusions of modern Anglo-American philosophy is that there is no sharp distinction between analytic truths and statements that are true only be virtue of the facts; what had been called analytic truths in earlier work, it is alleged, are simply expressions of deeply held belief. This conclusion seems quite erroneous. There is no fact about the world that I could discover that would convince me that you persuaded John to go to college even though he never intended or decided to go to college; nor is there any fact of experience even relevant to the judgment that you failed to persuade him if he never intended or decided to go to college. The relation between *persuadir* ("persuade") and *tener intención* ("intend") or *decidir* ("decide") is one of conceptual structure, independent of experience—though experience is necessary to determine which labels a particular language uses for the concepts that enter into such relations. The philosophical debate over these matters has been misleading because it has focused on very simple examples, examples involving words that lack the relational structure of such terms as *chase* and *persuade*. Thus there is much debate over whether the statement "Cats are animals" is a truth of meaning or of fact (if we discovered that what we call cats are really robots controlled by Martians, would the sentence "Cats are animals" now be considered false, or would we conclude that what we have called cats are not really cats?). In such cases a decision is not easy to reach, but in others it seems quite straightforward.

Furthermore, empirical inquiry can help clarify the status of a statement as a truth of meaning or of empirical fact; for example, inquiry into language acquisition and variation among languages. Thus the distinction between truths of meaning and truths of empirical fact is an empirical issue, not to be decided merely by reflection or, certainly, by stipulation. The whole matter requires extensive rethinking, and much of what has been generally assumed for the past several decades about these questions appears to be dubious at best.

It seems that the child approaches the task of acquiring a language with a rich conceptual framework already in place and also with a rich system of assumptions about sound structure and the structure of more complex utterances. These constitute the parts of our knowledge that come "from the original hand of nature," in Hume's phrase. They constitute one part of the human biological endowment, to be awakened by experience and to be sharpened and enriched in the course of the child's interactions with the human and material world. In these terms we can approach a solution of Plato's problem, along lines not entirely unlike Plato's own, though "purged of the error of preexistence." I will come back in the last lecture to further questions that arise as we consider these conclusions and their implications.

The Research Program of Modern Linguistics

Yesterday I discussed some of the basic questions of the science of language. We may pose the central problem of this inquiry in the following terms. The human mind/brain is a complex system with various interacting components, one of which we may call the language faculty. This system appears to be unique in essentials to the human species and common to members of the species. Presented with data, the language faculty determines a particular language: Spanish, English, etc. This language in turn determines a wide range of potential phenomena going far beyond the presented data. Schematically, then, we have the following picture:

(1)
data → | language faculty | → language → structured expressions

Suppose that a child with the human language faculty as a part of its innate endowment is placed in a social environment in which Spanish is spoken. The language faculty selects relevant data from the events taking place in the environment; making use of these data in a manner determined by its internal structure, the child constructs a language, Spanish, or more properly the variety of Spanish to which it is exposed. This language is now incorporated in the mind. When the process is completed, the language constitutes the mature state attained by the language faculty. The person now speaks and understands this language.

The language now constitutes one of the many systems of knowledge that the person has come to acquire, one of the person's cognitive systems. The language is a rich and complex system of some sort, with specific properties that are determined by the nature of the mind/brain. This language in turn determines a vast range of potential phenomena; it assigns a structure to linguistic expressions that go far beyond any experience. If the language is Spanish, then the cognitive system that the child has acquired determines that *strid* is not a possible word; the same is true if the language is Arabic, but not English. Similarly, the language determines that the phrase *el libro* can be used with a concrete or an abstract sense or both simultaneously. It determines connections of meaning between the word *persuadir* and the phrase *tener intención*. It determines further that *Juan se hizo afeitar* is a properly formed sentence with its specific meaning, although this status is lost, in violation of various analogies, if we add *a los muchachos* to the end of the sentence or *a quién* to the beginning of the sentence. And so on, for an unlimited range of possible phenomena that far transcend the experience of the person who has acquired the language or the speech community that this person joins.

I should mention that I am using the term "language" to refer to an *individual* phenomenon, a system represented in the mind/brain of a particular individual. If we could investigate in sufficient detail, we would find that no two individuals share exactly the same language in this sense, even identical twins who grow up in the same social environment. Two individuals can communicate to the extent that their languages are sufficiently similar.

37   In ordinary usage, in contrast, when we speak of a language, we have in mind some kind of *social* phenomenon, a shared property of a community. What kind of community? There is no clear answer to this question. We speak of Chinese as a language, whereas Spanish, Catalan, Portuguese, Italian, and the other Romance languages are different languages. But the so-called dialects of Chinese are as varied as the Romance languages. We call Dutch a language and German a different language, but the variety of German spoken near the Dutch border can be understood by speakers of Dutch who live nearby, though not by speakers of German in more remote areas. The term "language" as used in ordinary discourse involves obscure sociopolitical and normative factors. It is doubtful that we can give a coherent account of how the term is actually used. This is not a problem for the ordinary use of language. Its conditions require only that usage be sufficiently clear for ordinary purposes. But in pursuing a serious inquiry into language, we require some conceptual precision and therefore must refine, modify, or simply replace the concepts of ordinary usage, just as physics assigns a precise technical meaning to such terms as "energy," "force," and "work," departing from the imprecise and rather obscure concepts of ordinary usage. It may be possible and worthwhile to undertake the study of language in its sociopolitical dimensions, but this further inquiry can proceed only to the extent that we have some grasp of the properties and principles of language in a narrower sense, in the sense of individual psychology. It will be a study of how the systems represented in the mind/brains of various interacting speakers differ and are related within a community characterized in part at least in nonlinguistic terms.

It is also worth bearing in mind that the language faculty does appear to be a unique human possession.

Other organisms have their own systems of communication, but these have properties radically different from human language, and human language is far more than a mere system of communication: Language is used for expression of thought, for establishing interpersonal relations with no particular concern for communication, for play, and for a variety of other human ends. In the past years there have been numerous efforts to teach other organisms (for example, chimpanzees and gorillas) some of the rudiments of human language, but it is now widely recognized that these efforts have failed, a fact that will hardly surprise anyone who gives some thought to the matter. The language faculty confers enormous advantages on a species that possesses it. It is hardly likely that some species has this capacity but has never thought to use it until instructed by humans. That is about as likely as the discovery that on some remote island there is a species of bird that is perfectly capable of flight but has never thought to fly until instructed by humans in this skill. Although not a logical impossibility, this would be a biological miracle, and there is no reason to suppose that it has taken place. Rather, as we should have expected all along, the evidence suggests that the most rudimentary features of human language are far beyond the capacity of otherwise intelligent apes, just as the capacity to fly or the homing instinct of pigeons lie beyond the capacity of humans.

The language faculty is not only unique to the human species in essentials, as far as we know, but also common to the species. We know of no reason to suspect that there is anything like racial differentiation in the language faculty. If there are genetic differences that affect the acquisition and use of language, they are well beyond our current capacity to detect them, apart from defects that affect much else as well. The language faculty functions in humans even under conditions of severe pathology and deprivation. Children afflicted with Down's syndrome (Mongoloids), who are incapable of many intellectual achievements, nevertheless appear to develop language in something like the normal manner, though at a much slower pace and within certain limits. Blind children suffer serious deprivation of experience, but their language faculty develops in a normal way. They even exhibit a remarkable capacity to use the visual vocabulary (such terms as "stare," "gaze," and "watch") in much the way that people with normal vision do. There are cases of people who have acquired the nuances and complexities of normal language, to a remarkable degree of sophistication, though they have been both blind and deaf from early childhood, from under two years old in some cases, a time when they were able to speak only a few words; their access to language is limited to the data they can obtain by placing their hand on the face of a speaking person (it may be significant, however, that none of the people who have succeeded in acquiring language in this way were deaf and blind from birth). Such examples illustrate that very limited data suffice for the language faculty of the mind/brain to provide a rich and complex language, with much of the detail and refinement of the language of people not similarly deprived. There are even examples of children who have created a system much like normal language without any experience with language at all—deaf children who had not been exposed to the use of visual symbols but who developed their own species of sign language, a language that has the essential properties of spoken languages but in a different medium.

These are fascinating topics that have been explored profitably in the past few years. The general conclusion that these studies seem to support is the one I have already stated: The language faculty appears to be a species property, common to the species and unique to it in its essentials, capable of producing a rich, highly articulated, and complex language on the basis of quite rudimentary data. The language that develops in this manner, largely along lines determined by our common biological nature, enters deeply into thought and understanding and forms an essential part of our nature.

To gain further understanding of these questions, we may return to the schematic description of acquisition of language outlined in (1). The goal of our inquiry is to determine the nature and properties of the languages acquired; then we can turn to Plato's problem, asking how this achievement is possible. The answer will lie in the properties of the language faculty, the system of (1) that converts the data available to the child into the language that comes to be incorporated in the mind/brain. We can then turn to further questions concerning language use and the physical mechanisms involved in the representation, use, and acquisition of language.

I have discussed a number of examples illustrating the problems that arise, and as we proceed, I will return to some possible answers to these problems. Let us first investigate further the problems that we face in this inquiry. As we proceed from simple to more complex cases, the argument and analysis will become more complex, and some care and attention will be necessary to follow it. I believe that this is necessary if one hopes to deal in a sensible way with general issues concerning language, thought, and knowledge, which have been the subject of a great deal of speculation, heated debate, and confident assertion over many centuries. I believe further that these discussions often suffer from a failure to perceive just what is involved in the growth and use of language and that familiarity with the facts of the matter would show that much of the discussion is misguided and seriously misconceived. I will try to support this judgment as we proceed. If it is correct, then the sometimes arduous and intellectually challenging task of pursuing the inquiry I will outline here—though only in rudimentary form—is worthwhile, indeed essential for anyone who hopes to gain a serious understanding of these more general topics. Imagine a Martian scientist, call him John M., who knows physics and the other natural sciences but knows nothing about human language. Suppose that he now discovers this curious biological phenomenon and seeks to understand it, pursuing the methods of the sciences, the methods of rational inquiry. Observing or experimenting with speakers of Spanish, John M. discovers that they produce such sentences as (2) and that they combine them into the more complex structure (3):

(2)
a. El hombre está en la casa.
The man is in the house.
"The man is at home."[1]
b. El hombre está contento.
"The man is happy."

(3)
El hombre, que está contento, está en la casa.
The man, who is happy, is in the house.
"The man, who is happy, is at home."

These are *declarative* sentences, making assertions that are true or false, as circumstances indicate.

Proceeding further, John M. discovers that Spanish speakers form *interrogative* sentences corresponding to the examples of (2) by moving the verb to the front of the sentence, yielding

---

1. Depending on dialect, the Spanish sentence may or may not mean "The man is at home" as well as the literal "The man is in the house." I keep to the former translation.

(4)
a. Está el hombre en la casa?
   Is the man in the house?
   "Is the man at home?"
b. Está el hombre contento?
   "Is the man happy?"

John M. now asks himself how to form an interrogative sentence corresponding to (3). This is a normal question of science. Evidently, speakers of Spanish have some rule that they use to form interrogatives corresponding to declaratives, some rule that forms part of the language incorporated in their mind/brain. The Martian scientist has certain evidence about the nature of this rule, namely, the evidence provided by examples such as (2) and (4). His problem is to construct a hypothesis as to what the rule is and to test it by looking at more complex examples, such as (3).

The obvious and most simple hypothesis is that the rule functions in this manner: Find the first occurrence of the verbal form *está* (or others like it), and move it to the front of the sentence. Let us call this rule R. Rule R applies to the examples of (2), yielding (4), in accordance with the observed facts.

Applying the hypothesis to the more complex example (3), we search the sentence from the beginning until we find the first occurrence of *está,* then place it in the front of the sentence, yielding the form

(5)
Está el hombre, que contento, está en la casa?
"Is the man, who happy, is at home?"

But this is gibberish, in Spanish as well as in English. The interrogative corresponding to (3) is not (5) but rather the form (6):

(6)

Está el hombre, que está contento, en la casa?
"Is the man, who is happy, at home?"

Discovering that his hypothesis has failed, the Martian scientist will now try to construct a different hypothesis to replace rule R. The simplest possibility is that the rule seeks the last occurrence of *está* and places it in the front of the sentence. This rule works for all the examples given so far, but it is plainly wrong, as he will quickly discover. Pursuing his inquiry further, John M. will discover that no rule that refers simply to the linear order of words of a sentence will work. The correct rule, of course, is the following: Find the occurrence of *está* (and similar words) that is the *main verb* of the sentence, the verb of its main clause, and place it in the front. Call this rule, the correct one, R-Q (the rule of question formation).

This is a surprising discovery, though the facts are entirely obvious to us. It is important to learn to be surprised by simple things—for example, by the fact that bodies fall down, not up, and that they fall at a certain rate; that if pushed, they move on a flat surface in a straight line, not a circle; and so on. The beginning of science is the recognition that the simplest phenomena of ordinary life raise quite serious problems: Why are they as they are, instead of some different way? In the case we are considering, the Martian scientist, John M., if a serious scientist, would be extremely surprised by what he has discovered. The actual rule, R-Q, is far more complex from a computational point of view than the rules that he has been forced to abandon. To apply these simpler rules, one must be able to identify words in sequence; to apply R-Q, one must undertake a complex computational analysis to discover a verb that is in a certain structural position in the sentence, situated among its phrases in a specific way. This is not a trivial computational task by any means. One may ask, then, why Spanish (and English) speakers use the computationally complex rule R-Q instead of the simpler rules that require attention only to the linear order of words. We face here a simple but fairly dramatic case of Plato's problem.

Having established that these are the facts about Spanish, John M. will then attempt to address Plato's problem: How do Spanish speakers know that they are to use the computationally complex rule R-Q, not the simple rule based on linear order? He might speculate that they are taught. Thus perhaps children proceed exactly as the scientist did in his inquiry. Observing such examples as (2) and (4), they hit upon the simple linear rule R and assume it to be the operative rule. Then, when they attempt to construct a question corresponding to (3), they form the construction (5) and are told by their parents that that is not the way we say things in Spanish; you should say (6) instead. After receiving sufficient instruction of this nature, children somehow succeed in devising the rule R-Q.

The Martian scientist will quickly discover that these speculations are incorrect. Children never make errors about such matters and receive no corrections or instruction about them. Similarly, no text written to teach Spanish to foreigners will warn the reader not to use the simple linear rule R but to use instead the computationally complex rule R-Q. In fact, until quite recently, no study of language even explicitly noticed that R-Q is used instead of the simple linear rule R; the fact was not considered interesting, just as in earlier stages of human science the rate of fall of a stone was not considered interesting.

Discovering all of this, the Martian scientist John M. would be left with only one plausible conclusion: Some innate principle of the mind/brain yields R-Q as the only possibility, given the simple data of (2) and (4). The simple linear rule R is never even available as a candidate to be considered. Investigating further, John M. will discover that all rules of Spanish, and of human language more generally, are similar to R-Q and unlike the linear rule R in a crucial formal respect. The rules of language do not consider simple linear order but are *structure dependent*, like R-Q. The rules operate on expressions that are assigned a certain structure in terms of a hierarchy of phrases of various types. For (2) and (3) the hierarchy can be expressed by placing phrases in brackets, as in (7) (where only some of the phrase structure is indicated):

(7)
a. [El hombre] está en la casa.
[The man] is at home.
b. [El hombre] está contento.
[The man] is happy.
c. [El hombre [que está contento]] está en la casa.
[The man [who is happy]] is at home.

The rule R-Q now finds the "most prominent" occurrence of *está,* the one that is not embedded within brackets in (7c), and places this occurrence of *está* at the front of the sentence, yielding the correct forms (4) and (6).

The child learning Spanish or any other human language knows, in advance of experience, that the rules will be structure dependent. The child does not consider the simple linear rule R, then discard it in favor of the more complex rule R-Q, in the manner of the rational scientist inquiring into language. Rather, the child knows without experience or instruction that the linear rule R is not a candidate and that the structure-dependent rule R-Q is the only possibility. This knowledge is part of the child's biological endowment, part of the structure of the language faculty. It forms part of the mental equipment with which the child faces the world of experience.

Notice that the task of the child learning Spanish and the task of the scientist inquiring into the nature of language, while similar in certain respects, are quite different in others. The principles that the scientist is trying to discover, the child already knows: intuitively, unconsciously, and beyond the possibility of conscious introspection. Therefore the child selects the rule R-Q at once, whereas the scientist must discover by an arduous process of inquiry and thought that R-Q is the operative rule of Spanish and that the principle of structure dependence is part of the structure of the language faculty, yielding the answer to Plato's problem in this case.

When the inquiring scientist is also a human being, with intuitive knowledge of language, the task is in some respects easier, in some respects not. Once the human scientist notices the problem just illustrated, the answer immediately springs to mind, because we can easily construct masses of relevant data and in fact are immersed in such data. In this respect the task of the human scientist is easier than that of the Martian, who does not know where to look, just as the human scientist does not know where to look when inquiring into the principles of physics. But intuitive understanding can also be a barrier to inquiry in that it can prevent us from even seeing that there is a problem to be solved. As I mentioned, until recently it was not realized that extremely simple facts such as those just reviewed constitute a problem at all.

Recall again that the facts are surprising. There is no logical reason why languages should use structure-dependent rather than linear rules. Languages can easily be constructed that use the computationally simpler linear rules. In such a language the question corresponding to (3) would be (5), not (6). This language would function perfectly well for the purposes of communication, expression of thought, or other uses of language. But it is not a human language. Children would have a hard time learning this simple language, whereas they learn the more complex human languages quite readily and without error or instruction in such cases as these because of their prior knowledge of human language and its principles. Similarly, mature speakers would find it difficult to use this formally much simpler language because they would have to carry out conscious computational operations instead of relying on the mechanisms provided by the language faculty, which operate automatically, without conscious thought. The principle of structure dependence is a significant, nontrivial property of human language, exhibited in such simple examples as these. This is an elementary illustration of the nature of Plato's problem and the way in which it can be approached and solved.

I have dwelt on this simple example at some length because it is both typical and instructive. It illustrates the fact that standard and familiar assumptions about the nature of language, and about the nature of mental capacities more generally, are quite wrong. It has long been supposed that organisms have certain general intellectual capacities, such as the capacity to carry out inductive reasoning, and that they apply these undifferentiated capacities to whatever intellectual task they may face. According to this view, humans differ from other animals in that they can apply these capacities more extensively; the same capacities are applied in general problem solving, science, games, language learning, and so on. Humans use "general learning mechanisms" to solve the tasks they face, and their systems of belief and knowledge arise in accordance with general principles of induction, habit formation, analogy, association, and so on.

But all of this is wrong, dramatically so, as we can see even from simple cases such as the one just reviewed. Evidently the language faculty incorporates quite specific principles that lie well beyond any "general learning mechanisms," and there is good reason to suppose that it is only one of a number of such special faculties of mind. It is, in fact, doubtful that "general learning mechanisms," if they exist, play a major part in the growth of our systems of knowledge and belief about the world in which we live—our cognitive systems. As we proceed further, we will find more and more evidence pointing in the same direction. The study of other animals yields similar conclusions about their capacities. It is fair to say that in any domain in which we have any understanding about the matter, specific and often highly structured capacities enter into the acquisition and use of belief and knowledge. Although we plainly can say nothing about matters that lie beyond our current understanding, it is difficult to see why one should retain the faith that traditional conceptions will somehow be applicable there, even though we find them generally useless to the extent that we come to understand some aspect of the nature of organisms, in particular, the mental life of humans.

Notice that it is not surprising that language has a hierarchical structure, as illustrated in the bracketing partially indicated in the examples given; many systems in nature, including biological systems and systems of cognition, have hierarchical structure of one or another sort. It is also no doubt possible to find examples of something like structure-dependent rules in domains other than language. But such observations are entirely beside the point here. Both linear rules such as R and structure-dependent rules such as R-Q are available for human mental processes. The question is why the child unerringly selects the computationally more complex structure-dependent rules in acquiring and using language, never considering the readily available and computationally much simpler linear rules. This is a property of the human language faculty, not a general property of biological organisms or of mental processes.

Let us turn to some more complex cases. Suppose that our Martian scientist continues his inquiry into Spanish, now asking how pronouns are used and interpreted. He will discover that pronouns come in two forms: the isolated form, such as *él*, and the clitic form, such as *lo*, attached to a verb in the manner of *se*, as in the examples I discussed in chapter 1. Thus he will find such sentences as (8a), with the isolated form *él* as the subject of the verb *ama*, and (8b), with the clitic form *lo* attached to the verb *examinar*, of which it is the direct object:

(8)
a. Él ama a Juan.
   He loves to Juan.
   "He loves Juan."
b. Juan nos mandó [examinarlo].
   Juan us-asked [to-examine-him].
   "Juan asked us to examine him."[2]

Sentence (8b) also has the clitic form *nos*, moved from the normal postverbal position of direct object of *mandar* and attached to the verb; thus (8b) illustrates the two possibilities for a clitic pronoun that we have seen in the alternative forms *Juan hizo afeitarse* and *Juan se hizo afeitar*.

Pronouns typically have two different uses. A pronoun such as *él* or *lo* can refer to some person whose identity is determined by the context of discourse, or its reference can be determined by some other phrase to which it is related. In the former case we say that the pronoun is *free*, in the latter case, *bound*. In (8b) *nos* is free, because there is nothing in the sentence to which it could be bound; but *lo* can be understood either as free or as bound by *Juan*, in which case it refers to Juan.

---

2. The clitic pronoun *lo* is ambiguously "him" or "it"; I keep to the former choice here. Elsewhere I keep to one meaning of ambiguous pronouns, choosing the interpretation relevant to the examples.

Discovering these facts, the Martian scientist would construct the natural hypothesis about the interpretation of pronouns: A pronoun can be free or bound, as illustrated in (8b). Turning to (8a), he would predict that *él* can be free, referring perhaps to some person Pedro, as determined by the discourse context, or bound, referring to Juan, so that the meaning of the sentence is "Juan se ama" ("Juan loves himself"). But his prediction is incorrect. In (8a) *él* must be free—its reference is not determined by the reference of *Juan*—though in other sentences, as he will quickly discover, *él* can be bound. Once again, a more complex hypothesis is required.

Note that we have another illustration of Plato's problem: The facts are known without experience or instruction and are surprising, in that the simplest hypothesis is incorrect.

The natural assumption, a stage more complex, is that the order of occurrence is what makes the difference. Because *lo* follows *Juan* in (8b), it can be bound by *Juan*, but because *él* precedes *Juan* in (8a), it cannot be bound by *Juan*. Again, the world has surprises. Consider the examples of (9):

(9)
a. [Su amigo] llamó a Juan.
   [His friend] called to Juan.
   "His friend called Juan."
b. [El hombre [que lo escribió]] destruyó el libro.
   [The man [that it-wrote]] destroyed the book.
   "The man who wrote it destroyed the book."

Here brackets demarcate the subject of the sentence, and in (9b) additional brackets demarcate the relative clause included within the subject.

In these sentences the pronoun *su* precedes *Juan* and *lo* precedes *el libro*. Hence, by the hypothesis we are considering, the pronouns cannot be bound by *Juan* and *el libro,* but must be free, referring to something other than Juan in (9a) and something other than the book that was destroyed in (9b). But this conclusion is false; the pronouns can be bound by *Juan* and *el libro.* The same is true of the English counterparts. Therefore the hypothesis is refuted, and the Martian scientist must seek some still more complex hypothesis.

He should, in fact, not be too surprised by the failure of the hypothesis, because again it relied on linear order and he had already found some reason to suspect that the rules of human language, surprisingly, do not seem to make essential use of this simple and prominent property but rather are structure dependent. Pursuing this insight in the present case, he might ask whether there is a structure-dependent interpretation of the facts about pronominal reference. Let us try the following idea.

Define the *domain* of a pronoun to be the smallest phrase in which it appears. Returning now to (8), we see that in (8a) the domain of *él* is the entire sentence, and in (8b) the domain of *lo* is the bracketed clausal fragment, which is the complement of the verb *mandó;* like the causative verb *hacer* discussed in the last lecture, the verb *mandar* takes a clausal complement, but *mandar* also takes a noun phrase complement, the clitic *nos* in (8b):

(8)
a. Él ama a Juan.
   "He loves Juan."

b. Juan nos mandó [examinarlo].
   Juan us-asked [to-examine-him].
   "Juan asked us to examine him."

In the English counterpart the verb *ask* also takes two complements, the noun phrase *us* and the clausal complement *to examine him.*

Turning to the more complex examples (9), we see that the domain of *su* in (9a) is *su amigo* and the domain of *lo* is certainly no larger than the embedded relative clause *que lo escribió* (in fact it is even smaller, as we will see directly):

(9)
a. [Su amigo] llamó a Juan.
   "[His friend] called Juan."
b. [El hombre [que lo escribió]] destruyó el libro.
   "[The man [who wrote it]] destroyed the book."

Consider now the following principle:

(10)
A pronoun must be free in its domain.

Turning to (8), we see that this principle implies that *él* must be free but *lo* can be bound by *Juan,* which is outside of its domain. In the case of (9) *su* may be bound by *Juan* and *lo* may be bound by *el libro,* because even if bound, each will be free in its domain. All cases are therefore covered by the structure-dependent principle (10)—in English as in Spanish.

Principle (10), which appears to be valid for human languages in general, belongs to a component of linguistic theory called *binding theory,* which is concerned with connections among noun phrases that have to do with such semantic properties as dependence of reference, including the connection between a pronoun and its *antecedent* (the connection between *lo* and *Juan* in (8), for example). This theory, which has interesting properties that are only partially understood, deals with one of the subparts of the language faculty. This subsystem interacts with others to yield an array of complex linguistic phenomena, some of which we will explore as we proceed.

Let us now dismiss the Martian scientist and proceed further on our own to investigate the properties of the language faculty. We continue as before, trying to discover surprising facts and seeking an explanation for them. We now assume principle (10) to be established and ask what we can learn by investigating how it applies in further cases.

Consider the sentence (11), with phrases demarcated by brackets as before:

(11)

[El hombre [que escribió el libro]] lo destruyó.
[The man [that wrote the book]] it-destroyed.
"The man who wrote the book destroyed it."

Can the pronoun *lo* be bound by *el libro* here? The answer is that it can, just as in the corresponding English sentence *it* can be bound by *the book*. We conclude, therefore, that *el libro* is not in the domain of *lo* and that in the corresponding English sentence *the book* is not in the domain of *it*. If the phrases were only as indicated in (11), the domain of *lo* would be the entire clause, so *el libro* would be in the domain of *lo*. Therefore there must be more structure than indicated. There must be a phrase including *lo* but excluding *el libro; that is, lo destruyó* must constitute a phrase, so that the structure is actually as in (12):

(12)

[El hombre [que escribió el libro]] [lo destruyó].
[The man [that wrote the book]] [it destroyed].
"[The man [who wrote the book]] [destroyed it]."

Assuming this structure, we can apply principle (10), permitting the reference of *lo* to be determined by *el libro,* to which *lo* is bound. Because the domain of *lo* in (12) is the phrase [*lo destruyó*], *lo* is free in its domain, satisfying principle (10), even if it is bound by *el libro*. The same reasoning holds for the English counterpart.

Sentence (12) is of the general form subject-verb-object, where the subject is *el hombre que escribió el libro* ("the man who wrote the book"), the verb is *destruyó* ("destroyed"), and the object is the pronoun *lo,* moved to the preverbal clitic position (in Spanish, although not in English, which lacks clitic pronouns). We see that there is an asymmetry between the subject and the object. The subject and the verb are in separate phrases, but the verb and the object form a single phrase, which we call a verb phrase. In general, then, subject-verb-object sentences have the form (13), where we now indicate the category of a phrase by a subscript on the bracket, NP for noun phrase, VP for verb phrase, and C for clause:

(13)

[$_C$ NP [$_{VP}$ V NP]]

There is a good deal of independent evidence converging on this conclusion, one piece of which I have just presented. It is, once again, by no means a necessary conclusion. One might assume that a transitive verb simply relates two terms, its subject and its object, with no asymmetry of structure. In fact, that is the assumption made in the construction of formal languages for the purposes of logic and mathematics, and it has often been proposed for human languages as well. Formal languages are constructed in this way for reasons of simplicity and ease in computational operations such as inference. But the evidence indicates that human languages do not adopt the principles familiar in modern logic. Rather, they adhere to the classical Aristotelian conception that a sentence has a subject and a predicate, where the predicate may be complex: It may consist of a verb and its object, as in (12) and (13), or a verb and a clausal complement, as in (8b).

This asymmetry, a property of human language but not a necessary property, is once again surprising. It gives rise to Plato's problem once again. How do children acquiring a language come to know this fact? It might be thought that they discover the fact as we just did, but that is certainly false. Our path of inquiry involved conscious inference based on the explicitly formulated principle (10), and we made use of evidence that is surely not generally available to the language learner. In fact, the line of argument just presented, which leads to general conclusions about the language faculty, would not be convincing unless it were supported by similar evidence from other languages as well, and the child does not have evidence from other languages available. Even within a single language it cannot be that the child hears such sentences as (12), discovers that the sentence can be used with *lo* bound by *el libro,* and then concludes that *lo destruyó* constitutes a verb phrase because if it does not, the principles of binding theory will be violated. Rather, as language grows in the mind/brain, the child comes to incorporate the principle that a transitive verb and its object form a phrase, as a matter of biological necessity; and then principle (10) of binding theory, which is part of the language faculty as a matter of biological necessity, determines the interpretation of such sentences as (12) by a computational process of unconscious inference.

The subject-object asymmetry has numerous consequences. Thus in some languages it is possible to form a complex verb by a process called incorporation: A noun may be added to the verb in the manner of a clitic pronoun in Spanish, forming a complex verb. In such languages, for example, from sentence (14a) we can derive (14b) with the complex verb *ciervo-caza:*

(14)
a. Juan caza los ciervos.
Juan hunts the deers.
"Juan hunts deer."

b. Juan ciervo-caza.
"Juan deer-hunts."

But it is not possible to form sentence (15), with the complex verb *Juan-caza* formed by incorporating the subject in the verb:

(15)
Juan-caza los ciervos.
"Juan-hunts deer."

Again, there is a subject-object asymmetry. The facts can be explained in terms of structure-dependent principles operating on phrase structure representations with the asymmetry of (13). For deep-seated reasons that go beyond what I can present here, the asymmetry of phrase structure representations entails that the object of a verb can incorporate within it to form a complex verb, but the subject cannot.

Such noun-incorporation constructions do not exist in Spanish, but we find something similar here as well. Consider causative constructions such as

(16)
a. Juan hace [que Pedro salga].
Juan makes [that Pedro leave].
"Juan makes Pedro leave."

b. [Que Juan mienta] hace que sus amigos desconfíen de él.
[That Juan lies] makes that his friends distrust of him."
"The fact that John lies causes his friends to distrust him."

A common feature of the causative construction in many languages is that a complex verb is formed from the causative element (in Spanish, *hacer*) and the verb of its complement. Thus from (16a) such a language could form the complex verb *hace-salir* ("make-leave"), so that the sentence would be (17), with a complex verb:

(17)

Juan hace-salir Pedro.

"Juan makes-leave Pedro."

But, although the verb of the complement of the causative verb can (and quite typically does) move to form a complex verb in this manner, the verb of the subject of the causative verb cannot. Thus no language can form a structure such as (18) from (16b) with the complex verb *hace-mentir:*

(18)

Juan hace-mentir que sus amigos desconfíen de él.

"Juan makes-lie that his friends distrust him."

Even in English, where no such constructions exist, there is some intuitive plausibility to the observation. Thus consider the constructions

(19)

a. Such problems cause [that governments lie].

"Such problems cause governments to lie."

b. [That governments lie] causes problems.

It is intuitively plausible that a language might have a word "lie-cause" that permits (19a) to be expressed as (20a) but does not permit (19b) to be expressed as (20b):

(20)

a. Such problems lie-cause governments.

b. Governments lie-cause problems.

Indeed, cross-linguistic evidence shows that this is correct.[3] Although no one has done the experiment, it is

---

3. Similar observations hold of the lexicon. Thus the word *drop* has some semantic relation to *cause to fall* so that "John dropped the book" means something like "John caused that the book fall" ("John caused the book to fall"). But there is no word *DROP* with the property that "the book DROPs problems" means something like "That the book falls causes problems."

probably the case that if English speakers were taught "pseudolanguages" with such verbs as *lie-cause*, they would more readily understand such constructions as (20a) meaning (19a) than such constructions as (20b) meaning (20a).[4]

We see here a reflection of the same asymmetry between subject and object. The verb and its complement are closely enough related so that the verb of the complement can attach to the main verb, forming a complex verb; but the verb of the subject cannot, because the subject does not form a phrase together with the main verb. The deeper reasons for these differences in incorporation possibilities are only now beginning to be understood, in work that lies beyond the scope of what I will be able to touch on here.

Notice that, although Spanish does not form a single complex word *hace-salir* as in (17), nevertheless something like the same process takes place in Spanish. We may assume that the abstract form directly underlying (17) is (21a), analogous to (16a), repeated here as (21b):

(21)
a. Juan hace [Pedro salir].
   "Juan makes [Pedro leave]."
b. Juan hace [que Pedro salga].
   Juan makes [that Pedro leave].
   "Juan causes Pedro to leave."

In (21a) the verb *salir* moves to the front of the embedded clause yielding (22a), which becomes the actual form

---

4. In designing such an experiment, one would have to be careful to ensure that it is tapping the resources of the language faculty, not the general problem-solving capacities, whatever they may be. As always, the design of a relevant experiment is not a trivial matter.

(22b) by the insertion of the proposition *a:*

(22)

a. Juan hace [salir Pedro].
   Juan makes [leave Pedro].

b. Juan hace [salir a Pedro].
   Juan makes [leave to Pedro].
   "Juan makes Pedro leave."

Although the order of subject and verb is fairly free in Spanish, in causative constructions such as (22) the verb of the complement clause must precede its subject in most dialects; it must be adjacent to the causative verb *hacer*. I will return to the insertion of the preposition. This aside, the fact that the verb moves to a position adjacent to the causative suggests that something similar to verb incorporation is also taking place in Spanish, and other evidence suggests that the two verbs that are adjacent become a single unit, *hacer-salir*. This would, for example, explain why the clitic *se* in *Juan se hizo afeitar* moves from its position as object of *afeitar* to attach to *hizo,* as if *hizo-afeitar* is functioning as a single verb. The phenomenon is much more general and is found throughout the Romance languages with some variation. As we will see, it is not just the verb of the complement clause that moves to the front, but a larger verb phrase, and the verb of this verb phrase then forms a functional unit with the causative verb *hacer* to which it is now adjacent.

These examples again illustrate the asymmetry of subject and object, a linguistic universal, it seems, with many effects. Once again, we should bear in mind that these are not logically necessary properties of language but rather facts about human language, traceable to properties of the language faculty. As in other cases the examples show that Plato's problem is a serious one and that we can hope to answer it by turning our attention to the

60   rich biological endowment that determines the language
faculty, one specific structure of the human mind.

Let us return now to the schematic account of the
process of language acquisition:

(1)

data → | language faculty | → language → structured expressions

In these terms we can outline a certain research program
for the study of language. The language faculty is a component of the mind/brain, part of the human biological
endowment. Presented with data, the child, or, more
specifically, the child's language faculty, forms a language,
a computational system of some kind that provides structured representations of linguistic expressions that determine their sound and meaning. The linguist's task is to
discover the nature of the elements of (1): the data, the
language faculty, the language, and the structured expressions determined by the language.

Still keeping to a schematic account, we can picture
the linguist's research as a process that begins at the right-
hand end of diagram (1) and works its way to an inquiry
into the nature of the language faculty. Research typically
begins with examples of structured expressions or, more
precisely, with judgments by speakers (or other evidence)
that suggest at least a partial account of the form and
meaning of these expressions and thus provide at least a
partial account of their structure. For example, examining
the Spanish speaker's understanding of (8), repeated here,
the linguist can determine that *lo* in (8b) may (or may
not) be bound by *Juan*, whereas in (8a) *él* may not be
bound by *Juan*:

(8)
a. Él ama a Juan.
   He loves to Juan.
   "He loves Juan."

b. Juan nos mandó [examinarlo].
Juan us-asked [to-examine-him].
"Juan asked us to examine him."

Similarly in other cases such as those we have discussed. Given an array of evidence of this sort, the linguist can turn to the next task: describing the language that determines these facts. At this stage, the linguist is attempting to construct a grammar of a particular language, that is, a theory of that language. If the grammar is sufficiently explicit—what is called a generative grammar—it will predict an unbounded range of structured expressions and can be tested for empirical adequacy by investigating the accuracy of these predictions. The linguist will undertake this task for as wide a range of languages as possible, attempting to construct for each an explicit grammar that will account for the phenomena at hand. This is a hard and demanding task. It is the task of describing a real object of the real world, the language that is represented in the mind/brain of the mature speaker of a language.

The next task is to explain why the facts are the way they are, facts of the sort we have reviewed, for example. This task of explanation leads to inquiry into the language faculty. A theory of the language faculty is sometimes called universal grammar, adapting a traditional term to a research program somewhat differently conceived. Universal grammar attempts to formulate the principles that enter into the operation of the language faculty. The grammar of a particular language is an account of the state of the language faculty after it has been presented with data of experience; universal grammar is an account of the initial state of the language faculty before any experience. It would include, for example, the principle that rules are structure dependent, that a pronoun must be free in its domain, that there is a subject-object asymmetry, some of the principles mentioned in the preceding lecture, and so on. Universal grammar provides a genuine explanation of observed phenomena. From its principles we can deduce that the phenomena must be of a certain character, not some different character, given the initial data that the language faculty used to achieve its current state. To the extent that we can construct a theory of universal grammar, we have a solution to Plato's problem in this domain.

Of course, this account is only schematic. In practice the various inquiries proceed in mutual interdependence. Thus, to the extent that we have some ideas about universal grammar, this will influence the way we assign structures to the expressions that constitute the evidence for research into descriptive grammar and it will influence the form of these descriptive grammars.

The principles of universal grammar are exceptionless, because they constitute the language faculty itself, a framework for any particular human language, the basis for the acquisition of language. But languages plainly differ. Returning to the schematic account (1), we see that the observed facts do not follow from the principles of the language faculty alone but from these principles in combination with the data presented to the language learner, which have determined various options left unsettled by universal grammar. In the technical terminology I introduced in chapter 1, the principles of universal grammar have certain *parameters,* which can be fixed by experience in one or another way. We may think of the language faculty as a complex and intricate network of some sort associated with a switch box consisting of an array of switches that can be in one of two positions. Unless the switches are set one way or another, the system does not function. When they are set in one of the permissible ways, then the system functions in accordance with its nature, but differently, depending on how the switches are set. The fixed network is the system of principles of universal grammar; the switches are the parameters to be fixed by experience. The data presented to the child learning the language must suffice to set the switches one way or another. When these switches are set, the child has command of a particular language and knows the facts of that language: that a particular expression has a particular meaning, and so on. Each permissible array of switch settings determines a particular language. Acquisition of a language is in part a process of setting the switches one way or another on the basis of the presented data, a process of fixing the values of the parameters.[5] Once these values are determined, the entire system functions, but there is no simple relation between the value selected for a parameter and the consequences of this choice as it works its way through the intricate system of universal grammar. It may turn out that the change of a few parameters, or even of one, yields a language that seems to be quite different in character from the original. Correspondingly, languages that are historically unrelated may be quite similar if they happen to have the same parameter settings.

The point can be illustrated with the Romance languages. Their historical separation is rather recent, and they are structurally quite similar. French, however, differs from the other Romance languages in a curious cluster of properties. In Spanish, for example, there are such constructions as

(23)
a. Llega.
   Arrives.
   "He/she/it arrives."

---

5. Note that this is only part of the story. In addition, we must consider acquisition of vocabulary items, idioms, irregular verbs, and so on. The discussion here is limited to what is sometimes called *core language,* in technical usage.

b. Llega Juan.
Arrives Juan.
"Juan arrives."

c. Lo quiere ver.
Him/it wants to-see.
"He/she wants to see him/it."

The same is true of Italian and other Romance languages. But in French the corresponding forms are impossible. The subject must be explicitly expressed throughout, and it cannot follow the verb as in (23b) (but the French causative form corresponding to (22b), *Juan hace [salir a Pedro]*, does have the verb-subject order, again indicating that the verb has moved to the beginning of the complement clause). And, although in Spanish the construction *querer-ver* acts more or less as a single compound verb so that the clitic object of *ver* can attach to *quiere* in (23c) (much in the manner of *hacer-afeitar,* as discussed earlier), this is not possible in French, where the clitic object must attach to the verb of the complement clause. These differences between French and the other Romance languages developed only a few centuries ago and apparently at about the same time. It is likely that they are consequences of a change in a single parameter, perhaps influenced by the example of the nearby Germanic languages. To establish this conclusion (assuming it to be correct), we would have to show that the structure of universal grammar dictates that a change in one parameter yields the observed cluster of effects. Some progress has been made in reducing these consequences to what is called the *null subject parameter,* which determines whether the subject of a clause can be suppressed, as in (23a), and there has been some interesting recent work on language acquisition exploring how the value of this parameter is determined in early childhood. But much remains unexplained. These are intriguing and difficult questions, just on the border of current research and only recently opened up for serious investigation with the progress of our understanding. The logic of the situation is something like what underlies the determination of biological species. The biology of life is rather similar in all species, from yeasts to humans. But small differences in such factors as the timing of cell mechanisms can produce large differences in the organism that results, the difference between a whale and a butterfly, for example. Similarly, the languages of the world appear to be radically different from one another in all sorts of respects, but we know that they must be cast from the same mold, that their essential properties must be determined by the fixed principles of universal grammar. If that were not so, it would not be possible for the child to learn any one of them.

The task of description is difficult enough, but the task of explanation, of developing universal grammar, is far harder and more challenging. At the descriptive level the linguist is presented with an array of phenomena and seeks to discover a computational system that will account for these phenomena and others that are predicted. At the explanatory level it is necessary to show how the phenomena can be derived from invariant principles once parameters are set. This is a far more difficult task. In the past few years it has become possible to approach this challenge and to make some real progress in coming to terms with it, to an extent that barely could be imagined not long before.

In the next lecture, I want to turn to a closer investigation of some of the principles and parameters of universal grammar, working up to an attempt to explain some of the phenomena that I have reviewed in the course of this discussion.

RESEARCH PROGRAM

Principles of Language Structure I

___

I concluded the last chapter with some remarks on the various levels of inquiry into language: first, the descriptive level, at which we attempt to exhibit the properties of particular languages, to give a precise account of the computational system that determines the form and meaning of linguistic expressions in these languages; and second, the explanatory level, at which we focus on the nature of the language faculty, its principles and parameters of variation. At the explanatory level we try to present the fixed and invariant system from which one can literally deduce the various possible human languages, including those that exist and many others, by setting the parameters in one of the permissible ways and showing what properties of linguistic expressions follow from these parameter settings. By setting the parameters one way, we deduce the properties of Hungarian; by setting them in another way, the properties of Eskimo; and so on. This is an exciting prospect. For the first time we are now in the position to envision it and to begin to undertake the project in a serious way.

I mentioned a few plausible principles of universal grammar and several parameters of variation, among them the null subject parameter that distinguishes French (and English, and many other languages) from Spanish and the other Romance languages (and a large variety of others). Pursuing the matter further, let us consider the nature of the categories and phrases that appear in the structured expressions of particular human languages.

Universal grammar permits certain categories of lexical items, basically four: verbs (V), nouns (N), adjectives (A), and adpositions (P; prepositions or postpositions, depending on whether they precede or follow their complements). These categories probably have an internal structure, but let us put that aside. The basic elements of the lexicon fall within these four categories, though there are others as well. For each of these basic categories, universal grammar provides a *projection* of which it is the *head*: verb phrase (VP), noun phrase (NP), adjective phrase (AP), adpositional phrase (PP). In Spanish, for example, as in English, we have the following four kinds of phrase:

(1)
a. VP: hablar inglés
   "speak English"
b. NP: traducción del libro
   translation of-the book
   "translation of the book"
c. AP: lleno de agua
   "full of water"
d. PP: a Juan
   "to Juan"

Each of these phrases has a head and its complement. The head in each case is a lexical category of the appropriate type, and the complement in each case is an NP (though other choices are possible; as we have seen, the verb *hacer* ("make") takes a clausal complement, and the verb *mandar* ("ask") takes both an NP and a clausal complement). The head of the VP in (1a) is the verb *hablar,* and its complement is the NP *inglés,* which happens to consist of a single noun in this case. The head of the NP in (1b) is

69   the noun *traducción,* and its complement is the NP *el libro;* the preposition *de* is inserted for reasons to which we will return, and the sequence *de-el* becomes the single form *del* by a rule of the sound system. The same is true of the AP in (1c), with the adjective *lleno* as its head and the NP *agua* its complement, and with *de* again inserted. The head of the PP in (1d) is the preposition *a,* and its complement is the NP *Juan.*

One striking fact about these constructions is that in each the head precedes its complements. The same is true in English. Other languages differ. Thus in Miskito, for example, the head follows the complement in each case, and the same is true of Japanese and others. But order aside, the general structure illustrated in (1) is an invariant core of language. If we let *X* and *Y* be variables that can take as their value any of the lexical categories V, N, A, P, then we can express the general structure of the phrase in the following formula:

(2)
$XP = X\text{-}YP$

We understand this formula to mean that for each choice of *X* (V, N, A, P) there is a phrase *XP* (VP, NP, AP, PP) with the lexical category *X* as its head and the phrase *YP* as its complement (where *YP* is the projection of some category *Y*, again in accordance with (2)). We understand the order of the head *X* and the complement *YP* to be free in the general formula (2).

Principle (2) belongs to universal grammar. Along with some others like it, it specifies the general properties of the phrases of a human language. As it stands, the principle does not yield actual phrases; it remains to fix the order of the head and complement and to provide the actual lexical items of the various lexical categories. Lexical items have to be individually learned, though as we saw in the first lecture, universal grammar imposes narrow conditions on their character and variety. The order of head and complement is one of the parameters of universal grammar, as we can see by comparing Spanish and Miskito, for example. In Spanish the value of the parameter is "head first"; each lexical head precedes its complement. In Miskito the value of the parameter is "head last"; each lexical head follows its complement. Miskito and Spanish are "mirror images" in this respect. In some languages the situation is more complex, and there may actually be more than one parameter involved, but this seems to be the core system in essence.

Notice that the value of the parameter is easily learned from short simple sentences. To set the value of the parameter for Spanish, for example, it suffices to observe three-word sentences such as

(3)
Juan [habla inglés].
"Juan [speaks English]."

Such evidence suffices to establish that the value of the parameter is head first and, in the absence of explicit evidence to the contrary, to establish the head-complement order throughout the language. The most crucial fact about language learning is that it proceeds on the basis of fairly simple data with no need for training or instruction or even correction of error on the part of the speech community; these are some of the features that give rise to Plato's problem. The head parameter, then, has the properties we expect to find throughout the system: Its value is readily learned, and once learned, it permits a system of general principles to function to determine a broad array of other facts.

Earlier we found evidence that in a subject-verb-object clause, there is a subject-object asymmetry in that the verb and the object form a single phrase, whereas the subject is a distinct phrase. Thus in (3) the structure is as indicated by the brackets, which demarcate a VP. The general principles of phrase structure provide further, more abstract evidence in favor of the conclusion that we reached earlier on the basis of considerations of binding theory and incorporation. If the conclusion holds, then we can maintain the general principle (2), whereas if there were no subject-object asymmetry, as in familiar formal languages, the general principle would be violated in the case of verbs; furthermore, it would simply be an accident that verb and object conform to the head-complement order in such languages as Spanish and Miskito. We therefore have a welcome convergence of empirical evidence and the theoretical desideratum of maintaining a general principle.

Some languages exhibit the verb-subject-object order, which appears to violate principle (2), whatever the value of the head parameter, because the verb and object are separated. For principle (2) to hold, it must be that, at a more abstract level of representation, the verb and the object form a single phrase. In fact, there is evidence that in such languages the basic structure of the clause is NP-VP and that the verb moves to the beginning of the clause, much as it does in Spanish causatives (4a), as we saw earlier, or in such sentences as (4b), where *regaló* also must appear at the beginning of the clause to which it belongs, or in the simple question form (4c):

(4)
a. Juan hizo [salir a Pedro].
 Juan made [leave to Pedro].
 "Juan made Pedro leave."

b. A quién no sabes qué libro [regaló Juan]?
 To whom not you-know what book [gave John]?
 "To whom don't you know what book John gave?"[1]

---

1. In some languages sentences such as (4b) are quite acceptable; in others, less so. English dialects vary in this respect. Spanish

c. Está Juan en la casa?
"Is Juan at home?"

The rule that moves the verbal element to the front is a general option permitted by universal grammar. It is used in somewhat different ways in different languages, and the situation in Spanish is a bit more complex than indicated here; thus in (4a) it is actually the verb phrase, not just the verb, that moves to the front, and in (4b) the moved element is also more complex than just the verb, as we see when we consider more complex examples. But again the apparent variety conceals a limited range of possible rules and structures among which the child finds its way as its mind/brain searches the data presented and sets the parameters, constructing a system of knowledge that enables the child to speak and understand the language of the speech community in its full complexity and richness.

Notice that some of the options made available by universal grammar may not be used in a particular language or may be used in only a limited way. To illustrate in another area of language, consider the difference in sound between the Spanish words *caro* ("expensive") and *carro* ("car"). Because English does not make use of this phonetic distinction, permitted by universal grammar, a speaker of English may have difficulty hearing the distinction. For the same reason the Spanish speaker may have difficulty hearing the difference between the English words *bat* and *vat,* because Spanish does not make use of this distinction. Universal grammar provides options within a rather restricted range. Not every option is fully used, or used at all, in every language.

---

and Italian typically accept such sentences more readily than many English or French dialects, it appears. There seems to be, then, a (rather minor) parameter of variation, one that has been studied in some recent work. There are further questions, which we will ignore, relating to semantic properties of the verb of the main clause.

There are possibilities of word order permitted by universal grammar that go beyond those I have illustrated. The languages mentioned so far observe the condition that the elements of a phrase are adjacent, at least in an underlying abstract structure that conforms to the phrase structure principles of (2), a structure that may be modified by such rules as verb movement. But some languages do not observe this condition of adjacency in the underlying abstract structure. Phrases may be genuinely "scattered," though there is good reason to believe that the phrases do exist and are determined by the same general principles with other forms of association replacing adjacency.

Such principles of phrase structure as (2) facilitate the task of learning language, because all that must be done is to set the value of the head parameter and others like it; the remainder of the system is then determined automatically. These principles also facilitate the task of perceiving and understanding what one hears, the perception aspect of question 3, p. 3, chapter 1. Suppose, for example, that a speaker of Spanish hears this sentence:

(5)
El hombre quiere el agua.
"The man wants the water."

Knowing the words and the value of the head parameter, it is at once possible to assign the structure (6), without reference to any specific rules of Spanish, using only principles of universal grammar:

(6)
[NP el hombre][VP quiere [NP el agua]]

The same is true of much more complex examples.

The principles of universal grammar are part of the fixed structure of the mind/brain, and it may be assumed that such mechanisms operate virtually instantaneously.

To the extent that sentence analysis relies on these principles, understanding should be virtually as fast as identification of vocabulary items. This appears to be the case, a fact that suggests that we are on the right track in seeking to reduce the "learned" component of language to the lexicon and the choice of values for a limited number of parameters.

Let us return to the pronominal system. As we have seen, here too, universal grammar provides several possibilities of variation among languages. Thus pronouns may be clitics, as in the case of one class of Spanish pronouns, but this option is not used in English. More intricate questions arise when we consider the binding of pronouns, as we have already seen. Let us return to the problems concerning the binding of the reflexive clitic *se,* illustrated in the first chapter but left without any solution. We are now in a position to investigate the topic somewhat more closely.

Consider the simplest case:

(7)
Juan se afeita.
Juan self-shaves.
"Juan shaves himself."

We know that the basic phrase structure parameter in Spanish is head first so that the verb *afeitar* must precede its object *se.* Hence the abstract underlying structure of (7), in which the principles of phrase structure and the parameter settings are observed, must be

(8)
Juan [afeita se].
Juan [shaves himself].

If we had chosen some other noun phrase instead of the reflexive, the order of (8) would be retained; and the preposition *a* would be inserted, a peculiarity of Spanish, as we have seen. But *se* is identified in the lexicon of Spanish as a clitic, so it must move in (8) to the preverbal position, where in effect it becomes part of the verb, yielding (7). It is an easily learnable property of Spanish that some pronouns, including *se,* are clitics; their behavior then follows from general principles of universal grammar.

There is a general and powerful principle of universal grammar, called the *projection principle,* that requires that the lexical properties of each lexical item must be preserved at every level of representation. The projection principle, which is supported by a wide variety of evidence, implies that the properties of *afeitar* must be represented at every level. The crucial lexical property of *afeitar* is that it is a transitive verb, requiring an object. This property is represented in (8) but not in (7), where the verb appears without an object. To satisfy the projection principle, (7) must have an object as well. Suppose, then, that universal grammar includes a principle stating that when an element moves, it leaves behind a *trace,* a category with no phonetic features that is bound by the moved element in something like the manner of a bound pronoun. The full structure of (7), then, is (9), where *t* is the trace of *se:*

(9)
Juan se [afeita *t*].

Here the trace *t* is the object of *afeitar* so that the projection principle is satisfied. There is substantial evidence that such traces exist in mental representation, some of which I will turn to directly. There is also evidence for the existence of other so-called *empty categories,* as we will see. Notice that none of this need be learned, because it reduces to properties of universal grammar.

Let us turn now to the causative reflexives that we investigated in the first chapter. Consider the sentence

(10)

Juan hizo [afeitarse a los muchachos].

Juan made [shave-self to the boys].

"Juan made the boys shave themselves."[2]

As we have seen, the underlying structure of (10) is (11), where the clause C is the complement of the causative verb *hizo:*

(11)

Juan hizo [$_C$ los muchachos [$_{VP}$ afeitar se]].

Juan made [$_C$ the boys [$_{VP}$ shave self]].

In this representation all the conditions of phrase structure, including the projection principle, are satisfied, and the value of the head parameter (head first) is satisfied as well. The clause C is the complement of *hacer,* with the NP *los muchachos* as its subject and the VP *afeitar se* as its VP predicate.

Because *se* is a clitic, it must attach to a verb. In (10) it attaches to *afeitar,* forming the complex verb *afeitarse.*[3] This form now moves to the front of its clause, a property of causative constructions as we have seen, yielding

(12)

Juan hizo [$_C$ afeitarse los muchachos].

Juan made [$_C$ shave-self the boys].

For reasons that we have not yet discussed, the preposition *a* is inserted before the NP *los muchachos,* giving the actual expressed form (10).

By virtue of its meaning, the clitic *se* must be bound. It cannot have independent reference but refers to someone specified elsewhere. It must have an antecedent,

---

2. Recall that the Spanish *se* is neutral with regard to number and gender; it can take either *Juan* or *los muchachos* as antecedent, structural conditions permitting.

3. To simplify the exposition, we ignore here the trace left by movement of *se,* which raises no problems in this case.

which determines its reference. We refer to an element that must be bound as an *anaphor*. However, *se* cannot select its antecedent freely. In (10), for example, *se* cannot refer to *Juan* but must refer to *los muchachos*. We can formulate the principle that determines the choice of antecedent in terms of the concept of *domain*, defined earlier: The domain of a phrase is the smallest phrase containing it. The anaphor *se* must be bound within the domain of a subject, in fact, the smallest such domain. We thus have a second principle of binding theory, in addition to principle (10) of chapter 2 stating that a pronoun must be free in its domain:

(13)
An anaphor must be bound within the minimal domain of a subject.

In sentence (10) the minimal domain of a subject is the clausal complement of *hizo;* this is the domain of the NP *los muchachos,* which is the subject of *afeitar.* Therefore *se* must be bound in this domain; it can take *los muchachos* as its subject but not *Juan,* which is outside this domain. Note that the same is true of corresponding English sentences, such as

(14)
Juan made [the boy shave himself].

Here the anaphor is *himself,* and the minimal domain of a subject containing *himself* is the phrase bounded with brackets, the subject being *the boy.* The anaphor *himself* must be bound within this domain, by virtue of principle (13). Therefore *himself* must be bound by *the boy,* not by *Juan.*

In both Spanish and English the reflexive anaphors in the constructions we are considering must be bound within the minimal domain of a subject. In English the reflexive anaphor *himself* may be bound by any element of this domain in an appropriate configuration, hence either the subject or the object within this domain. But in Spanish there are some further constraints. In certain constructions the reflexive element is necessarily bound by the subject of the domain in which it must find its antecedent. The possibilities are illustrated in (15a), where *himself* can take either the subject *Juan* or the object *Pedro* as its antecedent, but not *Mario,* because *Mario* is outside of the minimal domain of a subject, demarcated by brackets. But in (15b), which is a fairly direct translation of (15a) into Spanish, the reflexive *sí mismo* (the nonclitic alternative to *se)* must take *Juan* as its antecedent, not *Pedro:*

(15)
a. Mario wants [Juan to speak to Pedro about himself].
b. Mario quiere que [Juan hable a Pedro de sí mismo].

Principle (13) also holds for pronouns, except that they must be bound where an anaphor is free. Thus alongside (13) we have another principle of binding theory:

(16)
A pronoun must be free in the minimal domain of a subject.

This principle is illustrated in the sentence

(17)
Juan lo afeita a él.
Juan him-shaves to him.
"Juan shaves him."

Here, *lo* and *el* in effect constitute a single discontinuous pronoun, so that principle (16) applies to them as a unit. Here the minimal domain of a subject is the entire clause (17), the domain of the subject *Juan.* Exactly as in the English counterpart, the pronominal form *lo-el* is necessarily free in (17), referring to someone other than Juan, someone whose identity is determined elsewhere in the discourse situation. Matters become more complex as we proceed to a wider range of examples, as the reader can discover by considering other cases, but I will keep to the simple forms of the binding theory principles for our purposes here.

Recall that the clitic *se* must attach to a verb, but in a causative construction it can attach either to the verb of which it is the object, as in (18a), or to the causative itself, as in (18b), with dialect variation as we have seen:[4]

(18)
a. Juan hizo afeitarse. . . .
b. Juan se hizo afeitar. . . .

We have just reviewed the binding of *se* in (18a), where ". . ." is replaced by *a los muchachos*. Let us turn now to (18b) as in

(19)
a. Juan se hizo [afeitar *t*].
Juan self-made [shave *t*].
"Juan had someone shave him (Juan)."
b. Juan se hizo [afeitar *t* a los muchachos].
Juan self-made [shave *t* to the boys].
"Juan had the boys shave him (Juan)."

Here the trace *t* indicates the position from which *se* has moved.

As we have already observed, expression (19a) is an acceptable sentence of Spanish, but (19b) is not. We are now in a position to explain this curious fact. In (19) there are two anaphors, two elements that must be bound: *se* and its trace *t*. By the principle of anaphor

---

4. To simplify exposition, I now abstract away from dialect variation, assuming an "idealized" language in which both forms are acceptable.

binding (13), each of these elements must be bound in the minimal domain of a subject. Furthermore, the trace *t* must be bound by *se*, and *se*, in turn, must be bound by some noun phrase. In (19a) the only subject present is *Juan*, so both *se* and its trace *t* must be bound in the domain of *Juan*. This condition is satisfied with *se* bound by *Juan* and *t* bound by *se*. (Observe that the anaphor *t* is bound within the minimal domain of a subject but not by the subject itself, just as in the case of the English example (15a).) Therefore the sentence satisfies the conditions of binding theory and receives its interpretation: *Se* is understood to be the object of *afeitar* by virtue of the position of its trace *t*, and it is bound by *Juan* by virtue of the position it occupies.

Turning to (19b), we see that *se* must be bound in the domain of the subject *Juan*, and its trace *t* must be bound by its antecedent *se* in the domain of the subject *los muchachos*, just as *se* itself was bound in this domain in sentence (10): *Juan hizo [afeitarse a los muchachos]*. There is no problem with regard to *se*, which is bound by *Juan* as required, but its trace *t* is not bound in the domain of *los muchachos*.[5] Rather, *t* is bound by *se*, which is outside the domain of *los muchachos*. Therefore the computational principles of the mind/brain fail to assign an interpretation to this sentence, and it is unintelligible.

Note that the same is true in corresponding English sentences, such as (14), repeated here:

(14)
Juan made [the boy shave himself].

In English the anaphor *himself* is not a clitic; it remains in place and there is no trace. But *himself* must be bound in

---

5. We are still putting aside the status of *a*, inserted for other reasons and not affecting these computations.

the domain of the subject *the boy,* just as the trace of *se* must be bound in the embedded clause of the corresponding Spanish sentence. Thus in (14) *himself* is bound by *the boy,* not by *Juan.* But the trace *t* of (19b) cannot be bound by the embedded subject *los muchachos* because it must be bound by the clitic *se.* Therefore the Spanish sentence receives no interpretation by the computational principles of the mind/brain. The thought cannot be expressed in this way in Spanish, where the clitic moves to the verb *hizo* of the main clause.

We see here direct evidence that the trace *t,* though not pronounced, is actually present in the mental representation of the sentence. It is "seen" by the mind as the mind computes the structure of the sentence, and it must therefore satisfy the binding principle for anaphors, but it is not pronounced by the vocal mechanisms because it contains no phonetic features. The trace is one of a number of empty categories that have the property that they appear in mental representations but are not pronounced; they are visible to the mechanisms of the mind but send no signal to the vocal mechanisms.

As we observed in the first chapter, the expression *Juan se hizo afeitar,* though a fine sentence in isolation, becomes unintelligible when we add *a los muchachos* to the end, yielding (19b), or when we add *a quién* to the beginning, yielding (20), with the obligatory change of word order:

(20)
A quién se hizo Juan afeitar?
To whom self-made Juan shave?
"Whom did Juan have shave him (Juan)?"[6]

---

6. In colloquial English, "Who did Juan have shave him?" For clarity of exposition I use the form *whom* instead of the (more natural) form *who* in these examples. We return later to the

However, the alternative form, with *se* attached to the verb *afeitar* as in (21), is not affected by addition of *a los muchachos* (see (10)) or *a quién,* as in (21):

(21)
A quién hizo Juan afeitarse?
To whom made John shave-self?
"Whom did Juan have shave himself?"

We have dealt with the case in which *a los muchachos* is added. Let us now consider the addition of the phrase *a quién* to *Juan hizo afeitarse.*

In (21) *se* is not bound by the physically closest subject *Juan* but by the more remote element *quién,* which is understood to be the subject of *afeitar.* Similarly, in the English translation, "Whom did Juan have shave himself?" the anaphor *himself* is not bound by the physically closest subject *Juan* but by the more remote element *whom,* which is understood as the subject of *shave;* we are asking for the identification of the person who shaved himself, and there is no relation between *himself* and *Juan.* We have accounted for the case of (19b) in terms of the principles of binding theory. What about (20) and (21)?

Notice that there are two problems to solve here. We must explain why the anaphor *se* is bound by the more remote subject in (21), not by the physically closest one; and we must explain why (20) receives no interpretation at all.

Let us begin with (21). The binding principles tell us that *se* must be bound in the minimal domain of a subject. The facts tell us that *se* is not bound by *Juan* but by *quién.* There is only one way for the principles and the facts to be compatible: It must be that *afeitar* has a sub-

---

question of why the subject has the case normally associated with the object.

ject related to *a quién,* which creates a domain in which *se* is bound. That is, the mental representation must be (22), where *t* is the trace of *a quién:*[7]

(22)
A quién hizo Juan [afeitarse *t*]?
To whom made Juan [shave-self *t*]?
"Whom did Juan have shave himself?"

Here the trace *t* occupies the same position as *a los muchachos* in (10), repeated here:

(10)
Juan hizo [afeitarse a los muchachos].

That is, the trace *t* is the subject of the bracketed embedded clause in (22), just as *los muchachos* is the subject of the bracketed embedded clause in (10). Just as *se* must be bound within the domain of *los muchachos* in (10), so it must be bound within the domain of *t* in (22).[8]

This conclusion makes perfect sense. Sentences (22) and (10) are in fact quite parallel in the way they are understood, except that in (22) we are asking for the identity of the subject of *afeitar,* whereas in (10) the subject is identified as *los muchachos.* In (22) the trace *t* is understood in the manner of a variable in logic or mathematics (elementary algebra, for example). In this sentence we are asking who is the person *x* with the following property: Juan caused that *x* shave someone—in fact, someone elsewhere identified in the sentence, because there is an anaphor, *se,* in this position and the anaphor must be bound. This interpretation of the sentence is given directly by the representation (22).

Given the quite natural representation (22), we can

---

7. Again, we suppress the trace of *se* to simplify exposition.
8. Notice that in both cases the preposition *a* is inserted, though in such a way as not to affect these computations.

explain the surprising fact that *se* appears to be bound by the remote element *quién* but not the closer element *Juan*. In fact, *se* is not bound by *quién* but rather by its trace *t*, the variable that is bound by *quién*. And because this trace is the subject of *afeitar*, it creates a domain in which *se* must be bound. Hence *se* cannot be bound by *Juan*, despite its physical proximity.

Notice that the same is true of the corresponding English example (22), repeated here:

(22)
Whom did Juan have shave himself?

The actual mental representation, as in the Spanish case, is (23), where *t* is the trace of *whom:*

(23)
Whom did Juan have [*t* shave himself]?

Here *t*, the trace of *whom*, is the subject of the clausal complement demarcated by brackets. The anaphor *himself* must be bound within the domain of this subject, hence within the brackets. The anaphor therefore takes the trace *t* as its antecedent, not *Juan*, though *Juan* is the closest potential antecedent in the physical form. Correspondingly, the meaning of the sentence is (24):

(24)
Who is the person *x* with the following property: Juan had *x* shave *x*.

If the anaphor *himself* were bound by the physically closest potential antecedent, *Juan*, the sentence would have the meaning (25):

(25)
Who is the person *x* with the following property: Juan had *x* shave Juan.

This is a fine meaning, but it is not expressed by sentence (22); rather it must be expressed by sentence (26a), with the mental representation (26b), *t* being the trace of *whom:*

(26)

a. Whom did Juan have shave him?

b. Whom did Juan have [*t* shave him]?

Here the pronoun *him* is free in the bracketed clause, which is the domain of the subject *t,* as required by binding principle (16). It may therefore be bound by *Juan,* which is sufficiently "remote" in the abstract representation (26b), despite the proximity of *Juan* to *him* in the physical form (26a).

Let us now review the properties of causative reflexives, examining the way they are constructed step by step. The abstract structures that underlie (22) and (10) are both of the form (27), where the NP is *los muchachos* in (10) and *quién* in (22):

(27)

Juan hizo [$_C$ NP [$_{VP}$ afeitar se]].

The computational principles of the mind now carry out a series of operations to yield the actual sentence. First, the VP *afeitar se* is moved to the front of its clause C following the general rule for causatives, which, as we saw, actually forms a kind of complex verb in some languages and even in a certain sense in Spanish. Next, the preposition *a* is added for reasons not yet explained. We now have the representation (28), where *a*-NP can be regarded just as an expanded NP:

(28)

Juan hizo [$_C$[$_{VP}$ afeitar se] a-NP].

Next the clitic *se* attaches to the verb, either to *afeitar* to form *afeitarse* or to *hizo,* forming *se hizo.* We therefore have two cases to consider.

Let us first take the case in which the clitic attaches to *afeitar,* forming *afeitarse.* The binding principle for anaphors requires that *se* take an NP as its antecedent in (28). If the NP is *los muchachos,* we have sentence (10). If the NP is *quién,* two more mental operations apply. First *a-quién* moves to the front of the sentence leaving a trace, which is the actual antecedent of *se,* and then *hizo* moves to the front of its clause, attracted by the question word *quién,* yielding (21), *A quién hizo Juan afeitarse?* with its interpretation.

That accounts for the properties of (21). What about (20), repeated here.

(20)
A quién se hizo Juan afeitar?

The underlying structure is again (27), and we form (28) as before. But now we select the second option for the clitic *se,* attaching it to *hizo* and leaving its trace t_{se}:

(29)
Juan se hizo [afeitar t_{se} a-NP].

If the NP is *los muchachos,* we have the sentence (19b), and, as we saw, this violates the principles of binding theory because the trace t_{se} is not bound by its antecedent *se* in the domain of the subject NP (= *los muchachos*). If the NP is *quién,* then it moves to the front of the sentence, leaving its trace $t_{quién}$, and induces the usual change of word order, yielding

(30)
A quién se hizo Juan [afeitar t_{se} $t_{quién}$]?

Because the two traces are empty categories that send no signal to the vocal mechanisms, what is pronounced is the expression (20). But the mind sees (30) and must interpret it in accordance with the principles of binding theory. The anaphor *se* poses no problem: It is bound by *Juan.* But the trace t_{se} is not bound in the domain of the subject $t_{quién}$, so the sentence receives no interpretation, as required. Does the trace $t_{quién}$ satisfy the principles of binding theory? One might argue that it does, because the minimal domain of a subject including this element is the entire sentence. But the correct answer is that this trace is not an anaphor and is therefore not subject to the binding principle for anaphors. The trace t_{se} is bound by the referential expression *se*, an anaphor that is assigned its reference by its antecedent *Juan*. But the trace $t_{quién}$ is a variable, bound not by a referential expression but by *quién*, which is not a referential expression but an element of the same logical category as *todos* ("all") or *algunos* ("some"). In sentences (31), for example, the NPs *todos* and *todos los muchachos* are not terms that refer:

(31)
a. Todos están en España.
"All are in Spain."
b. Todos los muchachos están en España.
"All the boys are in Spain."

Rather, the meaning of these expressions is expressed more precisely by assuming that the logical structure is of the form (32), where x is a variable and *todos* and *todos los muchachos* are expressions specifying how broadly the variable may range in its interpretation:

(32)
a. Todos x, x están en España.
All x, x are in Spain.
b. Todos los muchachos x, x están en España.
All the boys x, x are in Spain.

In (32a) x ranges over all things (where the discourse situation indicates how broadly this is to be construed), and in (32b) x ranges over all the boys. Sentence (32b), then, asserts that, if we select any boy, that boy is in Spain.

Similarly, the logical structures of sentences (33) are essentially as indicated in (34):

(33)
a. Quiénes están en España?
   "Who are in Spain?"
b. Cuáles muchachos están en España?
   "Which boys are in Spain?"

(34)
a. Cuáles x, x están en España?
   Which x, x are in Spain?
b. Cuáles muchachos x, x están en España?
   Which boys x, x are in Spain?

In (34a) x again ranges over all things (as determined by the discourse situation); we are asking which of these things is in Spain. And in (34b) x ranges over all the boys. Sentence (33b) asks of which boys is it true that they are in Spain. In these cases the referential expression is not *quiénes* or *cuáles muchachos* but rather the variable x, which functions as a place holder for a true referential expression; the expression *Juan y Pedro* ("Juan and Pedro"), for example, which could fill the position of x in (34), is one possible answer to questions (33). The actual mental representation of (33) after the question phrases are moved to the beginning of the clause leaving the trace t would be

(35)
a. Quiénes [t están en España]?
   Who [t are in Spain]?
b. Cuáles muchachos [t están en España]?
   Which boys [t are in Spain]?

In (33) we see no overt physical evidence of movement because the question phrase has moved from the subject position, which happens to be at the beginning of the sentence in these cases. If the question phrase initially occupied some other position, as in (22), (30), or (36), we have overt evidence for movement:

(36)

a. Quiénes crees que [*t* están en España]?
Who you-think that [*t* are in Spain]?
"Who do you think are in Spain?"

b. Cuáles muchachos crees que [*t* están en España]?
Which boys you-think that [*t* are in Spain]?
"Which boys do you think are in Spain?"

There is strong evidence, however, that there is movement to the front in all cases, leaving a trace, even when the movement is "invisible." In all cases the trace *t* functions as a variable, in the manner of the logical representation (34), which is virtually identical with the syntactic representation (35). There is, incidentally, good evidence that something similar is true of the expressions (32) with *todos* instead of a question word, but I do not pursue this matter here.

In other words, terms such as *quién* are not referential expressions but *operators* that bind variables, which function as referential expressions. For the purposes of binding theory, the trace of an operator such as *quién*, functioning as a variable, is therefore regarded as a referential expression, not an anaphor. It is the variable *t*, left behind as *quién* or *cuáles muchachos* moved to the preclausal position, that assumes the semantic role assigned by the verb. In contrast, the trace of the clitic *se* merely transfers the semantic role to its antecedent, the referential expression that binds the trace (and that, in the case of *se*, has its reference determined in turn by its antecedent).

All of this makes sense from a logical point of view, and it is a fact of some interest that a natural logical structure is directly represented in the mental representations that underlie the actual expressions of language. Once again, this is not a logical necessity. One can easily construct languages that behave quite differently but would be no less satisfactory for the functions served by human language; these would not, however, be human languages. The human mind works in its own specific manner, constructing mental representations that happen to reflect quite directly the structures of certain logical systems. We see evidence for this conclusion in the way that the binding principles operate, as just illustrated.

We now have evidence for the presence of two traces in mental representation: the trace of *se* and the trace of *a quién*. The trace of *a quién* establishes a domain within which the trace of *se* must be bound. If the trace of *se* is not bound within this domain, as in *a quién se hizo Juan afeitar?* then the sentence receives no interpretation.

The computations just reviewed and the representations that they form and modify have the same claim to reality as other constructs of science: chemical elements, valence, molecules, atoms, and so on. They enter into the explanation of curious and complex phenomena, and we can look forward to the discovery of physical mechanisms that have the properties brought to light in this inquiry into the functioning of the human mind/brain.

The existence of empty categories is particularly interesting. The child learning a language has no direct evidence about them because they are not pronounced. But it seems that the child's language faculty incorporates quite precise knowledge of their properties. The child's mind places these empty categories where they belong, making use of the projection principle, and then determines their properties by applying various principles of universal grammar. The computations involved may be fairly intricate, as illustrated even by the simple examples we have discussed. But since they rely on principles of universal grammar that are part of the fixed structure of the mind/

brain, it is fair to suppose that they take place virtually instantaneously and of course with no conscious awareness and beyond the level of possible introspection. In these respects these computations are similar to the complex calculations of the mind/brain that inform me that I am seeing a group of people sitting in a lecture hall, though the actual visual information that my eye receives is limited and chaotic. As the seventeenth-century British philosopher Ralph Cudworth observed: "The book of nature is legible only to an intellectual eye."

Knowledge of the properties of empty categories is part of the framework that the human mind brings to the problem of language acquisition. The elements of this framework are not learned and could not be learned by the child in the time available and on the evidence available—it is no simple matter for the scientist inquiring into language to discover that these elements exist and to determine their properties, and this task requires a broad range of evidence not available to the child, including evidence from a variety of languages and evidence acquired by sustained empirical inquiry informed by complex theory construction. The knowledge that is incorporated in the human language faculty enters into the way we understand sentences in quite subtle ways, as these few simple examples have indicated.

The discovery of empty categories and the principles that govern them and that determine the nature of mental representations and computations in general may be compared with the discovery of waves, particles, genes, valence, and so on and the principles that hold of them, in the physical sciences. The same is true of the principles of phrase structure, binding theory, and other subsystems of universal grammar. We are beginning to see into the deeper hidden nature of the mind and to understand how it works, really for the first time in history, though the topics have been studied for literally thousands of years, often intensively and productively. It is possible that in the study of the mind/brain we are approaching a situation that is comparable with the physical sciences in the seventeenth century, when the great scientific revolution took place that laid the basis for the extraordinary accomplishments of subsequent years and determined much of the course of civilization since.

Principles of Language Structure II

In the last chapter I discussed how the mind determines the structure of examples ranging from very simple ones, such as *El hombre quiere el agua,* to somewhat more complex cases, such as *A quién hizo Juan afeitarse?* and *A quién se hizo Juan afeitar?* In the latter case mental processing runs into a contradiction and breaks down. Remember that these computations are carried out without any use of rules for the particular language or for particular constructions. Rather, the mind makes use of general principles of universal grammar and certain values for parameters and, of course, the meanings of particular words. These resources should suffice to determine the form and meaning of any sentence.

The computation is virtually instantaneous in examples such as those discussed and is unconscious and inaccessible to consciousness or introspection. In more complex cases what happens seems to be different, and is well beyond our understanding. It is easy to construct examples that offer a real challenge to the speaker of a language, who may have no clear idea at first about the way they should be interpreted or may interpret them wrongly, that is, not in accordance with the structure determined by the speaker's knowledge. Notice that there is no contradiction when we say that the mind/brain assigns an interpretation that differs from the structure determined by

94   the language faculty or fails to assign a structure determined by the language faculty. The actual use of language
involves elements of the mind/brain that go beyond the
language faculty, so what the speaker perceives or produces may not precisely reflect the properties of the language faculty taken in isolation.

In cases such as these, where speakers of a language
have no clear idea of what an expression means or are
informed that their interpretation is not the correct one,
the speakers "think about the expression" (whatever this
means), and after a period of reflection a conclusion
springs to mind about the meaning of the expression. All
of this, again, lies far beyond consciousness, and we have
no understanding at all about what the mind/brain is doing during this process, though we can observe its results.

Let us now review the main points discussed earlier
by moving on to examples that are a bit more intricate.
Consider the sentence

(1)
[El] hombre al que María nos quiere ver examinar] está
esperando.
[The man to whom Maria us-wants see examine] is
waiting.
"The man whom Mary wants to see us examine is
waiting."

Let us investigate the phrase in brackets, the subject of the
sentence, and ask how it is interpreted and why. We may
approach the question by thinking through the process by
which this sentence is interpreted by the mind/brain, assuming the principles so far discussed.

The first task is to identify the words and assign them
to their categories, making use of the resources of the lexicon, one component of the language that the person has
acquired in the manner briefly discussed in earlier chapters. Having identified the words, the mind then uses the

principles of phrase structure, with the parameters fixed for Spanish, to determine the general structure of the expression. Keeping just to the NP subject, its structure would in part be as follows, where the brackets demarcate a clausal element, identified for reference with the subscript C_1:

(2)

El hombre al que [$_{C_1}$ María nos quiere ver examinar].

Let us now take a closer look at C_1.

The word *quiere* ("wants") is a verb that takes a clausal complement, which follows it because the head parameter has the value head first. Hence we know that *ver examinar* is a clause C_2. Furthermore, *ver* ("see") is a verb that takes a clausal complement, which follows it by virtue of the head parameter; call it the clause C_3, which has the physical form *examinar* ("examine"). The principles of phrase structure therefore assign to C_1 the preliminary structure (3):

(3)

[$_{C_1}$ María nos quiere [$_{C_2}$ ver [$_{C_3}$ examinar]]].

The verb *examinar* requires an object, and by the projection principle this object must appear in the mental representation. Since it is not physically present, it must appear as an empty category. One possibility is that this empty category is essentially a pronoun, an empty category referring to someone unspecified. Let us put this possibility aside for the moment. The other possibility is that this empty category is the trace of some element that appears elsewhere; call it t_1. The subject of the clause C_3 is also not physically present. It is therefore missing altogether, or it is present as an empty category. Assuming the latter option, one possibility is that it also is a trace; call it t_2. Making this further assumption, the mind therefore assigns to (2) the further structure (4):

(4)

El hombre al que $[_{C_1}$ María nos quiere $[_{C_2}$ ver $[_{C_3}[_{VP}$ examinar $t_1]t_2]]]$.

Although I do not pursue the matter here, the subject trace t_2 does follow the VP in C_3, as indicated in (4), because the verb *ver* is rather like *hacer,* inducing movement of the VP to the front of the clause in the manner already discussed.

The structure (4) thus contains two traces, each of which requires an antecedent. It also contains two phrases that must bind a trace for the construction to receive an interpretation: the displaced clitic *nos* and the phrase *al que* (with the preposition *a* added as usual), a phrase that must bind a variable much as the corresponding question phrase must.

One of the traces must be bound by *nos* and the other by *al que*. Terms such as quantifier phrases or *al que,* which introduces a relative clause, we have called *operators.* Operators are not referential expressions but rather bind variables that function as the referential expressions and receive the semantic roles assigned within the clause. Sometimes the operator may not be physically present, but we have good reason to suppose that whenever there is a variable, there is an operator, possibly overt as in (4), possibly an empty category, a possibility that I do not explore here.

We may now incidentally discard the possibility that the subject of C_3 was missing altogether or that in place of t_1 we had an empty pronoun, because if this is so, either *nos* or *al que* would not have a trace as required and the sentence would receive no interpretation. The possibility of an empty pronoun instead of t_1 would, however, be realized in a sentence such as (5), in which *nos* moves from the position of subject of *examinar* and the object of *examinar* is a pronominal empty category, the interpretation being roughly that he wants to see us as we examine someone or other:

(5)
Quiere vernos examinar.
He/she-wants see-us examine.
"He/she wants to see us examine someone."

The option is permitted in (5) but not in (2), because (2) contains two phrases that must bind a trace. Note that the option is not available in English, which does not allow "empty pronouns" in the manner permitted in Spanish.

Returning to the analysis of (2), we now have to ask how the traces are bound. Suppose that t_1 is bound by *nos* and that t_2 is the variable bound by the operator *al que*. The analysis constructed by the mind would then be (6), where t_{nos} is the trace of *nos* and t_{que} is the trace of *al que*:

(6)
El hombre al que [$_{C_1}$ María nos quiere [$_{C_2}$ ver [$_{C_3}$ [$_{VP}$ examinar t_{nos}]t_{que}]]].

This analysis is impossible, however, because it violates the binding principle for anaphors: t_{nos} is an anaphor, but it is not bound by its antecedent *nos* in the minimal domain of a subject, namely C_3, which is the domain of the subject t_{que}. Therefore this interpretation is excluded.

The only other possibility is that t_1 is bound by the operator *al que* and t_2 by *nos*, as in

(7)
El hombre al que [$_{C_1}$ María nos quiere [$_{C_2}$ ver [$_{C_3}$[$_{VP}$ examinar t_{que}]t_{nos}]]].

The interpretation is that we are examining the man, not that the man is examining us. Now the binding of t_{nos} is legitimate because there is no domain of a subject including t_{nos} and excluding *nos*. And since t_{que} is a variable bound by the operator *al que*, not an anaphor, it is not subject to the binding condition for anaphors, as we observed earlier. Therefore the analysis constructed by the mind must be (7), all other options having been excluded.

In short, phrase (2), repeated here, must be understood with *nos* taken to be the subject of *examinar* in (2), not its object, and with the *a*-phrase *al que* taken to be the object of *examinar,* not its subject:

(2)

El hombre al que [$_{C_1}$ María nos quiere ver examinar].

Thus (2) must be understood in the manner of (8a), not (8b) (where *lo* stands for *el hombre*):

(8)
a. María quiere vérnoslo examinar.
María wants to-see-us-him examine.
"María wants to see us examine him."
b. María quiere verlo examinarnos.
María wants to-see-him examine-us.
"María wants to see him examine us."

The specific interpretation assigned to (2) is determined by a series of mental computations carried out by the language faculty in accordance with its fixed principles, making use of information provided by the choice of parameters and the lexical properties that are specific to Spanish (though again, selected within a narrowly circumscribed range). The computations involved in determining the meaning of (2) are moderately complex. At several points in the computation more than one option is available, but only one is selected because others lead to the violation of general principles of universal grammar, and the path to the correct analysis involves quite a few steps. Nevertheless, all of this proceeds virtually instantaneously and obviously without any conscious awareness or even the possibility of conscious awareness. The reason is that

99

the computation makes use of the fixed mechanisms of mind, set to operate in a specific way by choice of language-particular parameters and lexical items with their semantic properties.

Such examples as (1) provide further evidence that traces exist in mental representation, seen by the mind but not pronounced by the vocal mechanism. We also see again that the mental representation of the expression corresponds to an analysis that makes sense from a logical point of view. The logical notions are embedded in our deepest nature, in the very form of our language and thought, which is presumably why we can understand some kinds of logical systems quite readily, whereas others are inaccessible to us without considerable effort and conscious understanding, if at all.

Examples of this sort do not exist in English because English lacks clitic pronouns and other relevant properties of Spanish. But the effects of the binding principle for anaphors can be seen in English constructions that do not exist in Spanish. Consider, for example, such English sentences as

(9)
a. John hurt himself.
b. Bill expected John to hurt himself.
c. I met the man who Bill expected to hurt himself.

(10)
a. John hurt him.
b. Bill expected John to hurt him.
c. I met the man who Bill expected to hurt him.

As we have seen, binding principles require that the reflexive anaphor *himself* be bound in the minimal domain of a subject and that pronouns be free in this domain. Thus in (9a) and (10a) *himself* is bound by *John* and *him* is not bound by *John;* rather, its reference must be determined elsewhere in the discourse. Turning to (9b) and (10b), we see that *himself* is necessarily bound by *John* and that *him* cannot be bound by *John;* it may be free, or it may be bound by *Bill.* These results follow from the binding principles, given the fact that the phrase *John to hurt him/himself* is the clausal complement of *expect* and is the domain of the subject *John.*

The interesting cases are the examples (9c) and (10c). Here *himself* cannot be bound by the "closest" subject, namely *Bill,* but *him* may be bound by *Bill,* contrary to expectations. The problem is resolved when we realize that, once again, there is an empty category subject of *hurt,* so that the mental representation to which the binding principles apply is in fact (11):

(11)
I met the man who Bill expected [*t* to hurt himself/him].

Here *t* is the trace of the operator *who;* the trace *t* is a variable, the subject of the bracketed embedded clause. The anaphor *himself* must be bound, and the pronoun *him* free, in the domain of the subject *t.* The interpretations then follow.

These examples, however, cannot be translated into Spanish, which lacks the corresponding constructions, just as the examples discussed earlier involving clitics cannot be translated into English, which lacks pronominal clitics. The languages look quite different in these respects, and Chinese, Japanese, Hungarian, American Indian languages, the native languages of Africa and Australia, and others look still more different. But they are all essentially the same in their basic structure, conforming to the principles of universal grammar but differing in the phonetic and syntactic (and less frequently, semantic) form of lexical items and in the choice of parameters.

Let us turn now to other components of the system of universal grammar. Consider a language such as Latin, which has a fairly rich case system, unlike Spanish or English, where case appears only in the pronominal system and then only in a rudimentary form. In a Latin sentence corresponding to the Spanish sentence (12), for example, the subject *el hombre* would appear with the nominative case, the object *un libro* would take the accusative case, and the indirect object *la mujer* would take the dative case:

(12)
El hombre dió un libro a la mujer.
"The man gave a book to the woman."

If all languages are essentially alike in their deeper essential nature, we would expect Spanish and English also to have a case system of this general sort. Since the case endings do not appear overtly, they should have something of the status of empty categories. They should be present to the mind but not produced by the voice or heard by the ear. There is, in fact, evidence that this assumption is correct. Let us now look into this matter.

Suppose that one component of universal grammar is *case theory*, a system that stands alongside of binding theory and other subsystems of the language faculty. One principle of case theory is that referential expressions must have case. The general theory of case determines how case is assigned, with some variation permitted as usual. Suppose that it works approximately in this way.

There are two basic kinds of clauses: finite and infinitival. We have finite clauses in (12) as well as in (9a) and the main clause of (9b), repeated here:

(9)
a. John hurt himself.
b. Bill expected [John to hurt himself].

The bracketed embedded clause of (9b) is infinitival. As we saw earlier, Spanish lacks constructions such as (9b), but we find similar infinitival forms in such constructions as the causative. Thus the main clause of (13) with the verb *hizo* is finite, and the complement of *hizo* in (13) is infinitival:[1]

(13)

María hizo [examinarnos al profesor].

Maria caused [to-examine-us to-the teacher].

"Maria caused the teacher to examine us."

Finite clauses can stand alone; infinitival clauses generally cannot.

A finite clause typically has an indication of tense and of subject-verb agreement. Thus the verb of a finite clause will indicate the tense of the clause and will agree with its subject in such features as person, number, and gender; the form of *hizo* in (13) specifies past tense, third person, and singular number. An infinitival clause typically lacks these elements. Let us assume that the tense-agreement element of a finite clause assigns nominative case to the subject, with which the verb agrees, so that the subject of a finite clause has nominative case but the subject of an infinitive lacks case (unless the language has some special device to assign case here, as Latin in fact does).

Assume further that a verb assigns accusative case to its object and that a preposition assigns oblique case (which may have one or another form) to its object. The case system may be richer and some further variety may appear, but let us take this to be the rudimentary struc-

---

1. I translate these now as full English infinitival constructions, instead of using the reduced form "Maria made (had) the teacher examine us," without *to,* as before, in order to simplify the exposition; the distinction is lacking in Spanish. For reasons not discussed here, the sentence is more natural with the clitic *le* adjoined to *hizo.*

ture of the case system. The cases may be overt, as generally in Latin, or hidden, as generally in Spanish and English, but we assume them to be present, in accordance with these general principles of case assignment, whether overt or hidden.

It follows from these assumptions that a referential NP cannot appear in a position that is assigned no case, for example, the position of subject of an infinitive. Returning to (13), recall that its underlying abstract form is (14), where the infinitival clause C is the complement of *hizo-caused:*

(14)
a. María hizo [$_C$ el profesor [$_{VP}$ examinar nos]].
b. María caused [$_C$ the teacher [$_{VP}$ to examine us]].

Here we see a difference between Spanish and English. In the English example (14b), the verb *cause* can assign case to the NP subject *the teacher* of the embedded clause, "crossing" the clause boundary [$_C$ . . .]. This is a rather unusual property, lacking in Spanish. It is this property that accounts for the fact that constructions such as (9b), repeated here, exist in English but not in Spanish:

(9b)
Bill expected [John to hurt himself].

English permits the verb *expect* (similarly, other epistemic verbs such as *believe*) to assign case freely across the clausal boundary. Spanish does not, so the construction (9b) cannot exist; the embedded clause would have to be finite in the corresponding Spanish construction, so that its subject can receive case.

Returning again to (14), we see that the sentence cannot appear in the form (a) in Spanish because the NP *el profesor,* the subject of the clause C, lacks case. Lacking the exceptional device just illustrated in English, Spanish must exploit other devices for the sentence (14a) to be expressible. As we saw, the VP *examinarnos* (formed by movement of the clitic *nos* to the verb) moves to the front of its clause, yielding the form

(15)

María hizo [examinarnos el profesor].

but the NP *el profesor,* the subject of *examinar,* still lacks case. In languages that lack actual case endings, prepositions are generally used to indicate case. Hence Spanish makes use of a vacuous preposition *a,* lacking any semantic content, to overcome the lack of case on *el profesor.* Inserting this vacuous preposition, we have the actual form (16), with a rule of the sound system shortening *a-el* to *al:*

(16)

María hizo examinarnos al profesor.

Here the preposition *a* functions as a case marker, not as a true independent preposition.

As we have seen, Spanish in fact also uses this vacuous preposition when the object of a verb is human, as in

(17)

Él ama a Juan.

He loves to Juan.

"He loves Juan."

This is a peculiarity of Spanish not duplicated in the other Romance languages. But the use of a vacuous preposition to "save" an expression that would otherwise violate case theory is a common device made available by universal grammar.

If an NP appears in the position of subject of infinitive, it must be assigned case in some special manner. One possibility, available for certain verbs in English, is case marking by the verb of the main clause, as in (14b)

and (9b). Another possibility is as just illustrated: A vacuous preposition may be inserted. In causative constructions this possibility is limited in the dialects we are considering to certain structural positions, namely, those where a true prepositional phrase would be acceptable— for example, the complement of a lexical category or a position adjoined to a verb phrase, as in (13), where the phrase *al profesor* is adjoined to the VP *examinarnos*. This is the kind of construction where true prepositional phrases could appear, as we saw in such forms as (18), discussed in the first chapter:

(18)
Juan se hizo [afeitar por el barbero].
Juan self-made [shave by the barber].
"Juan had the barber shave him (Juan)."

In the adjoined phrase *por el barbero*, the preposition *por* is not vacuous but has a definite meaning; the phrase is a true prepositional phrase, not a noun phrase to which a preposition is added to satisfy the demands of case theory.

But prepositional phrases do not generally appear in subject position. Hence in most dialects we cannot "save" the expression (14a), repeated here as (19a) by simply inserting the vacuous preposition *a*, yielding (19b):

(19)
a. María hizo [el profesor [$_{VP}$ examinar nos]].
b. María hizo [al profesor examinarnos].

In (19a) the verb *hizo* permits the VP of its complement to move to the beginning of its clause. If a construction does not allow this movement, we cannot overcome the violation of case theory in this manner. Thus the verb *creer* does not permit fronting of the VP of its complement. For example, the principles of universal grammar permit us to construct an underlying abstract form such as (20), analogous in form to (14):

(20)
Creo [Juan estar enfermo].
I-believe [Juan to be sick].
"I believe Juan to be sick."

Here, however, the verb phrase *estar enfermo* of the complement clause cannot be moved to the front of its clause with the subject then receiving the case-marking preposition *a*, as in the case of (14). Furthermore, as already noted, Spanish lacks the device available in English that allows the subject *Juan* of the embedded clause to receive accusative case from the main verb *believe*, across the clause boundary, so that the abstract form can be realized directly. Therefore the legitimate abstract expression (20) cannot be realized as an actual sentence at all in Spanish. The option (21a), analogous to (16), is excluded, and (21b) is excluded as well in the dialects we are considering because prepositional phrases are barred from the subject position:

(21)
a. Creo [estar enfermo a Juan].
   I-believe [to be sick to Juan].
   "I believe Juan to be sick."
b. Creo [a Juan estar enfermo].
   I-believe [to Juan to be sick].

We might say that the thought expressed by (20), though properly constructed at the abstract level, cannot be expressed with an infinitival complement to *creer* in Spanish, though it can in English because in the construction corresponding to (20), *Juan* can be treated as the object of *believe* and assigned accusative case.

Consideration of the full range of structures and dialects suggests that other principles are actually operative here, but I keep to this special case.

Sometimes, there are other ways to "save" the construction permitted at the abstract level by universal grammar. Consider the sentence (22):[2]

(22)
Juan parece conocerlo bien a él.
Juan seems to-know-him well to him.
"Juan seems to know him well."

What is the semantic role of *Juan* in this construction? Plainly it is not functioning as the semantic subject of *parecer* ("seems"), because this verb does not assign any semantic role to its subject. Rather, as the sense makes clear, *Juan* is functioning as the subject of the verb *conocer* ("know"). Let us ask why this should be the case.

The verb *parecer* takes a clausal complement. The thought expressed in (22) could be expressed by the construction (23), in which *parecer* appears with a finite clause as its complement:

(23)
Parece que [Juan lo conoce bien a él].
It-seems that [Juan him-knows well to him].
"It seems that Juan knows him well."

Clauses can be either finite or infinitival, so alongside of (23), universal grammar provides the construction (24), with an infinitival complement to *parecer:*

(24)
Parece [Juan concerlo bien a él].
It-seems [Juan to-know-him well to him].
"It seems [Juan to know him well]."

The different positions of the clitic *lo* in (23) and (24) are normal for finite versus infinitival forms of the verb. In fact, (24) expresses approximately the same meaning as (23).

---

2. Notice that here we have the "discontinuous" pronominal form *lo-él*, as in examples discussed earlier.

Although (23) is an acceptable sentence, (24) is not, for reasons we already know: *Juan* receives no case. Notice that in this case the sentence cannot be "saved" in English because the verb *seem,* unlike *expect* or *believe,* does not have an accusative case to assign: We have such sentences as "I expected that" and "I believe that," but not "It seems that." The verb phrase *concerlo bien a él* cannot move to the front of its clause in this construction, and the subject *Juan* cannot be assigned the vacuous preposition *a* where it stands, as we have seen. The only way for (24) to escape the violation of case theory is for *Juan* to move to some position in which case is assigned. In fact, there is such a position: the subject of *parecer.* This position is not occupied in the abstract underlying structure provided by universal grammar, because *parecer* assigns no meaning to this position and, as we have seen throughout, the abstract underlying forms of linguistic expressions are projections of the lexical items, as determined by their semantic properties and the general principles of universal grammar (with parameters fixed). Since the position of subject of *parecer* is unoccupied, *Juan* can move there leaving the trace *t,* as in other cases we have discussed, yielding the form

(25)
Juan parece [*t* conocerlo bien a él].
Juan seems [*t* to-know-him well to him].
"Juan seems to know him well."

The mental representation of the corresponding English form will also have a trace, after movement of *Juan* to the main clause subject position, as in

(26)
Juan seems [*t* to know him well].

The trace *t* is an anaphor, just as the trace of a moved clitic is an anaphor, so it must satisfy the binding principle for anaphors. It must be bound in the minimal domain of a subject, namely, the domain of *Juan,* that is, the clauses (25) and (26) as a whole. Since it is bound in this domain, namely by *Juan,* binding theory is satisfied. Case theory is also satisfied, since *Juan* is assigned nominative case in this position. In fact, all principles of universal grammar are satisfied, so (25) is a properly formed sentence, pronounced as (22) because the trace is "invisible" to the vocal mechanism. The representation (25) and (26) is what is constructed and interpreted by the mind, as before, so that *Juan* is understood to be the subject of *conocer* (*know*) by virtue of the position of the trace that it binds. Here we see another way in which it is possible to escape the violation of case theory.

Notice that the grammar of Spanish and English contains no rule of "raising" that moves *Juan* from its abstract position in (24) to the position of subject of *parecer* (*seem*). In fact, we have so far not appealed to any rules at all in discussing the form and interpretation of sentences. Construction (22), corresponding to (23) in interpretation but different from it in form, is determined in both its sound and meaning by the interaction of various principles of universal grammar, the lexical items with their meanings, and the parameters set with their Spanish and English values.

We might ask why sentence (20), repeated here, cannot be "saved" by raising *Juan* to the subject position, to yield (27):

(20)
Creo [Juan estar enfermo].
I-believe [Juan to be sick.]

(27)
Juan creo [*t* estar enfermo.]
Juan I-believe [*t* to be sick].

That would be impossible here because of the disagreement in person between *Juan* and the first person verb *creo*. But even if the verb of (20) were *cree* ("thinks," third person), not *creo*, so there would be no disagreement in person, the operation must be blocked. The resulting sentence (28) is a properly formed expression but with an entirely different meaning; it does not assert that someone believes that Juan is sick:

(28)
Juan cree estar enfermo.
Juan believes to be sick.

We return to the status of (28) and the reasons why raising of *Juan* to the subject position in this case is barred.

Recall that the general theory of phrase structure permits a head to take a complement, which might (but need not) be a noun phrase; the complement follows the head in Spanish because of the value of the head parameter. In the last chapter I illustrated these possibilities with the examples

(29)
a. VP: hablar inglés
   "speak English"
b. NP: traducción del libro
   "translation of the book"
c. AP: lleno de agua.
   "full of water"
d. PP: a Juan
   "to Juan"

But universal grammar actually provides not the set of forms (29) but rather (30), where brackets demarcate the noun phrase complement of the head:

(30)

a. VP: hablar [inglés]
   speak [English]

b. NP: traducción [el libro]
   translation [the book]

c. AP: lleno [agua]
   full [water]

d. PP: a [Juan]
   to [Juan]

We are now in a position to explain the discrepancy between the predicted forms (30) and the actual forms (29). Verbs and prepositions assign case; nouns and adjectives do not. Hence, for the abstract forms of (30) to appear, case must somehow be assigned to the complement. Spanish again uses the device of inserting a vacuous preposition, in this case the preposition *de*, which has no independent meaning here but simply functions as a case marker, assigning oblique case to its object. English does the same, using the semantically empty preposition *of*. Hence the forms that actually appear are those of (29).

The function of the vacuous preposition can also be observed in the case of "intransitive prepositions" that do not require objects and correspondingly do not assign case, for example, *alrededor*, as in the following question-and-answer discourse:

(31)

a. Había gente alrededor?
   "Were there people around?"

b. Sí. Había gente alrededor de la casa.
   "Yes. There were people around the house."

In the answer the vacuous preposition *de* is inserted to assign case to *la casa;* the answer could not have been *Había gente alrededor la casa.* The reason lies in case theory; *alrededor* does not assign case, so a case marker must be introduced to "save" the construction *alrededor* [*la casa*], a P-NP construction permitted by universal grammar.[3] Consideration of a wider range of languages and of other more complex constructions suggests that this analysis is not quite correct and that the true story is that case theory includes another principle of case assignment: Nouns and adjectives (and perhaps intransitive prepositions) assign genitive case to their complements, this being one of the variants of oblique case. If so, then *de* is still a case marker, but it is the genitive case marker, as in *el libro de Juan* ("the book of Juan," "Juan's book"). That would explain why the vacuous preposition is *de* rather than *a* in these constructions (and *of* in English). There are other considerations, too complex to introduce here, that support this conclusion. In any event no specific rules are required to account for the apparent asymmetry that we observe in the forms (29).

Notice again the effects of the slight differences in values of parameters that distinguish Spanish from English. In both languages, for example, the abstract form of a causative reflexive would be (32), with appropriate choices of lexical items:

(32)
a. Juan hizo [$_C$ los muchachos [afeitar se]].
b. Juan made [$_C$ the boys [shave themselves]].

Lexical items apart, the two constructions are identical.

In English, sentence (32b) appears in exactly this form. This is permitted because the reflexive *themselves* is not a clitic but an independent word and because English

---

3. Note that English and Spanish differ in lexical properties of the words *alrededor* and *around,* which does assign case in English. A parallel English example would be *out,* as in "I left the example out," "I left the example out of my talk," but not "I left the example out my talk."

allows the subject of the embedded clause C (*the boys*) to be regarded for the purposes of case assignment as the object of the main verb *made,* the causative verb. But in Spanish this option is not available, and *se* is a clitic. Therefore other processes apply, as we have seen: First, the clitic *se* attaches to *afeitar* to form *afeitarse* (attachment to *hizo* being impermissible here for reasons of binding theory, as we have seen); next, the VP *afeitarse* moves to the beginning of the embedded clause C; and then the vacuous preposition *a* is introduced to yield finally

(33)
Juan hizo afeitarse a los muchachos.
Juan made shave-self to the boys.
"Juan made the boys shave themselves."

Superficially, the form (33) of Spanish appears to be quite different from the corresponding construction (32b) of English, but essentially they are the same, deriving from the same underlying structure determined by universal grammar. The differences result from the automatic operation of principles of universal grammar, when the parameters are set and lexical properties are brought into consideration. Much the same is true when we turn to languages of widely different kinds.

As we have seen, variables function as referential expressions for the purposes of binding theory, and the same is true with regard to case theory, a fact that supports our earlier conclusions about the status of variables. Thus variables must have case, just as ordinary referential expressions, such as *Juan* or *los muchachos,* must have case. We can illustrate the fact by considering the abstract forms (34) provided by universal grammar:

(34)
a. Parece [quiénes conocerlo bien a él].
   It-seems [who to-know-him well to him].

b. Parece [cuáles muchachos conocerlo bien a él].
It seems [which boys to-know-him well to him].

Suppose now that we move the operator phrase to the beginning of the sentence, as usual, forming the corresponding constructions (35), with *t* the trace of the moved operator:

(35)
a. Quiénes parece [*t* conocerlo bien a él]?
Who (plural) it-seems [*t* to-know-him well to him]?
"Who does it seem to know him well?"
b. Cuáles muchachos parece [*t* conocerlo bien a él]?
Which boys it-seems [*t* to-know-him well to him]?
"Which boys does it seem to know him well?"

But these are not properly formed questions. The reason lies in case theory: The trace *t* is a variable here as we have seen and therefore must have case; but case is not assigned in the position of the subject of the infinitive, so sentences (35) violate case theory.

Consider in contrast the sentence (25), repeated here:

(25)
Juan parece [*t* conocerlo bien a él].
"Juan seems [*t* to know him well]."

This sentence is properly formed, as distinct from those of (35), which are not. The reason is that in (35), the trace is a variable requiring case, whereas in (25) it is an anaphor bound by the referential NP *Juan* in subject position and thus does not require case because it is not itself a referential expression.

We know that *quiénes* and *cuáles muchachos* are not in the subject position in (35) but precede the entire clause, as distinct from *Juan* in (25), because of the failure of agreement with the singular verb *parece*. The point is still more obvious in the English counterparts, where the subject *it* explicitly appears.

In (34) the complement of *parece* is an infinitival clause. Universal grammar also permits a finite clausal complement in this position. If this option is selected, as in (36), we would derive the forms (37) by moving the operator phrase to the beginning of the main clause, as usual, where *t* is the unpronounced trace of the operator:

(36)
a. Parece que [quiénes lo conocen bien a él.]
It-seems that [who him-know well to him].
"It seems that [who know him well]."
b. Parece que [cuáles muchachos lo conocen bien a él].
It-seems that [which boys him-know well to him].
"It seems that [which boys know him well]."

(37)
a. Quiénes parece que [*t* lo conocen bien a él]?
Who (plural) it-seems that [*t* him-know well to him]?
"Who does it seem know him well?"
b. Cuáles muchachos parece que [*t* lo conocen bien a él]?
Which boys it-seems that [*t* him-know well to him]?
"Which boys does it seem know him well?"

These sentences are properly formed questions, as distinct from (34). The reason is that in (37) the variable *t* receives case, namely nominative case, as subject to the verb *conocen* ("know") of the finite clause.

We see again that there is good evidence that empty categories exist, with quite definite and specific properties.

We have identified two empty categories: the trace of an operator that is outside the clausal structure (as in (38)) and the trace of an NP that occupies a position within the clause (as in (39)):

(38)
a. A quién afeita Juan *t*?
To whom shaves Juan *t*?
Whom does Juan shave?

b. El hombre al que Juan afeita *t*.
   the man to whom Juan shaves *t*.
   "the man whom Juan shaves."

(39)
a. Juan se afeita *t*.
   Juan self-shaves *t*.
   "Juan shaves himself."
b. Juan parece [*t* estar enfermo].
   Juan seems [*t* to be sick].
   "Juan seems to be sick."

The variables of (38) function as referential expressions; they assume the semantic role assigned by *afeitar* ("shave") and must receive case. The traces in (39) are quite different. They do not assume the semantic roles assigned to the position they occupy but rather transfer them to their antecedents: *se* and *Juan,* respectively.

We can say that the antecedent and the trace constitute a *chain,* which is an abstract representation of the referential expression. The chain (*Juan, t*) in (39b) is an abstract representation of *Juan.* The chain receives case in the position occupied by its head, *Juan,* and it receives its semantic role in the position occupied by the trace *t*. To be properly formed, a chain must include a case-marked position (its head) and a position that is assigned a semantic role (the position occupied by the head in the abstract underlying structure). Furthermore, assignment of case and of semantic role to a chain must be unique or else the element occupying its head position, which the chain represents in an abstract manner, will not be properly identified with unique case and uniquely specified semantic properties. The chain must contain a unique position that is case marked and a unique position that receives a semantic role: its initial and final positions, respectively.

It follows, then, that a phrase can never move to a position that has a semantic role assigned to it or else the resulting chain will have two such positions: the position that the phrase initially occupied and the position to which it has now moved. These natural requirements narrowly constrain the possibilities of movement. In fact, they limit movement either to a position outside the clause, as in the case of an operator leaving a trace functioning as a variable, or to the subject position of a verb such as *parecer* ("seem"), which assigns no semantic role to its subject. The only other possibility, exemplified in clitic movement, is adjunction of an item to another element; in this case the item moves to a position to which no semantic role is assigned.

The same conditions hold for clitic chains, such as (*se, t*) in (39a), if we assume that case is actually assigned to the clitic itself, not its trace, an assumption that is reasonable on other grounds.

Let us return now to sentence (28), repeated here:

(28)
Juan cree estar enfermo.
Juan believes to be sick.

We observed that this sentence cannot have the structure (40), derived by raising from (41):

(40)
Juan cree [*t* estar enfermo].
Juan believes [*t* to be sick].

(41)
Cree [Juan estar enfermo].
It-believes [Juan to be sick].

The reason why raising is impossible in this case is that the chain (*Juan, t*) in (40) has two positions to which a semantic role is assigned: the subject of *cree* and the subject of *estar*. Hence the condition on chains is violated. Sentence (28) is properly formed in Spanish (though not in English) but with a different structure, to which we will turn shortly.

A variable, by virtue of its status as a referential expression, may head a chain, as in the construction (42):

(42)
Quiénes [parecen [t conocerlo bien a él]]?
Who [seem [t to-know-him well to him]]?
"Who seem to know him well?"

In contrast to (35a), repeated here, (42) is a properly formed expression:

(35a)
Quiénes [parece [t conocerlo bien a él]]?
Who [it-seems [t to-know-him well to him]]?

The reason why (35a) is not properly formed is that *quiénes* has moved directly from the position occupied by *t* to the preclausal position, leaving the trace *t* in a position that is not case marked, a violation of case theory as we have seen. We know that this was the course of the derivation, because the verb *parece* is singular, not plural; hence the plural form *quiénes* is not its subject. But in (42), the verb *parecen* is plural in number, so it must have a plural subject. It must be, then, that *quiénes* has moved from its original position, leaving the trace *t*, to the position of subject of *parecen*. Being an operator, it then moves to the preclausal position, leaving the trace *t'*. The structure of (42) is therefore actually (43):

(43)
Quiénes [c *t'* parecen [t conocerlo bien a él]]?
Who (plural) [c *t'* seem [t to-know-him well to him]]?
"Who seem to know him well?"

The derivation internal to the clause C is exactly as in the formation of (25):

(25)

Juan parece [*t* conocerlo bien a él].

"Juan seems [*t* to know him well]."

The position of *t'* in (43) is the same as that of *Juan* in (25). The trace *t'* in (43) is a variable, heading the chain (*t'*, *t*). This is a properly formed chain, receiving case in the position of its head *t'* and assigned its semantic role in the position of *t*. Being a variable, the head of the chain, *t'*, is bound by an operator, namely *quiénes*.

We also find examples of chains in the passive construction. Consider the abstract form (44), permitted by universal grammar:

(44)

Ha sido [devorada la oveja] [por el lobo].

It-has been [devoured the sheep] [by the wolf].

"The sheep has been devoured by the wolf."

Here *la oveja* is the object of the verb *devorar*. The object may move to the unoccupied subject position, yielding (45) and forming the chain (*la oveja*, *t*), which is assigned case in the position of its head and assigned its semantic role in the position of the trace:

(45)

La oveja ha sido [devorada *t*] [por el lobo].

"The sheep has been [devoured *t*] [by the wolf]."

In English or French the movement of the object to the subject position is obligatory; in Spanish or Italian it is optional. This difference follows from the value of the null subject parameter by virtue of properties of case theory. Essentially the point is that the passive form never assigns case (in fact, it may be that the passive element, functioning as the unexpressed subject, receives the case assigned by the verb, leaving no case to be assigned to the object). Hence the object of a passive must receive case in some other way. In English or French the object must move to a case-marked position, but in a language such as Spanish or Italian that permits the subject to be an empty category, this empty category can "transfer" its nominative case to the object so that the object need not appear in the position to which nominative case is assigned.

Suppose that instead of (45), we had the corresponding infinitival construction (46) as the complement of *parecer:*

(46)
parece [la oveja haber sido [devorada *t*] [por el lobo]].
It-seems [the sheep to have been [devoured *t*] [by the wolf]].

Here the chain (*la oveja, t*) (in English, (*the sheep, t*)) lacks case, so its head *la oveja* must move to a case-marked position, forming

(47)
La oveja parece [*t'* haber sido [devorada *t*] [por el lobo]].
The sheep seems [*t'* to have been [devoured *t*] [by the wolf]].

Here we have the three-termed chain (*la oveja, t', t*). Case is assigned to *la oveja* in the position of the head of the chain, and the semantic role is assigned to the final position of the chain, occupied by *t*.

There are other kinds of empty categories in addition to traces of the two types illustrated in the foregoing discussion. Consider the verb *hope,* which takes a clausal complement, expressing the content of the desire. This clausal complement, as usual, can be finite or infinitival, as in

(48)
a. They hoped that [they would finish the meeting happy].

b. They hoped [to finish the meeting happy].

Correspondingly in Spanish, we have such expressions as

(49)

a. Ellos esperaban que [publicarían el artículo contentos].
"They hoped that [they would publish the article happy]."

b. Ellos esperaban [publicar el artículo contentos].
"They hoped [to publish the article happy]."

In (48) and (49), the adjective *happy* (*contentos*) appears to modify the pronoun *they* (*ellos*); in the Spanish case the adjective also agrees in number (plural) with the subject *ellos*. But an adjective cannot modify and agree with a noun that is outside of its clause, as we can see from such expressions as

(50)

They hoped that [the meeting would finish happy].

(51)

Ellos esparaban que [el artículo se publicara contentos].
They hoped that [the article itself-would-get-published happy (plural)].
"They hoped that the article would get published happy."

In sentence (50) the adjective *happy* no longer modifies *they* but rather *the meeting;* their hope is that the meeting would end in a happy atmosphere, not that they would be happy. The English translation of (51) has only the senseless interpretation that their hope is that the article will be happy upon publication. The corresponding Spanish examples have no interpretation because the plural adjective *contentos* cannot modify the singular subject of the embedded clause. As the examples illustrate, the adjective of the embedded clause cannot modify an NP outside of this clause. In the examples of (48) and (49), the content of their desire is, roughly, that they will be happy when the meeting has ended and when the article is published, but this desire cannot be expressed by sentence (51).

Examples of this kind illustrate the fact that an adjective must be "close enough" to the noun it modifies. It can modify the subject of its own clause, as in *Ellos están contentos* ("They are happy"), but it cannot modify the subject of a different clause, as in (50) and (51). It follows, then, that there must be a subject in the complement clauses of (48) and (49). In example (48a) the subject of the complement clause is expressed: It is *they*. But in (48b) and the two cases of (49), it is not expressed. Because the subject is not expressed, it must be an empty category. Let us call the empty category that appears as the subject of the finite clause *pro* and the empty category that appears as the subject of the infinitive *PRO;* thus we have *pro* as the subject of (49a) and *PRO* as the subject of (48b) and (49b). As we will see, these have quite different properties, and both differ in their properties from the two kinds of trace.

The actual mental representation of the sentences of (48) and (49) is therefore (52) and (53), repectively:

(52)
a. They hoped that [they would finish the meeting happy].
b. They hoped [*PRO* to finish the meeting happy].

(53)
a. Ellos esperaban que [*pro* publicarían el artículo contentos].
b. Ellos esperaban [*PRO* publicar el artículo contentos].

The adjective *happy* (*contentos*) modifies the subject of its clause, as required.[4] In (53a) *pro* is simply an unpro-

---

4. Note that this corresponds to the meaning. The content of their hope, in (52), is that they will finish the meeting happy.

123 nounced pronoun. It is the "null subject" permitted in languages such as Spanish and Italian but not French and English, a parametric difference that, as we have seen, entails numerous consequences. It can appear as the case-marked subject of a finite verb and also perhaps elsewhere (for example, as the object of the verb *examinar*, as mentioned in connection with sentence (5)). It is interpreted in the manner of the overt pronoun, though there are some subtle differences. In (53a) *pro* can be free, so that *ellos* and *pro* refer to different groups of people as the discourse situation determines, or *pro* can be bound by *ellos*, referring to whatever people the overt pronoun *ellos* refers to. In these respects *pro* is exactly like an overt pronoun.

The empty category *PRO* in (52b) and (53b) is quite different. It is not a freely referring expression such as *the boys, they,* or Spanish *pro*. Rather, it typically has one of two uses: Either it is bound, or, if there is no available antecedent to bind it, it refers to something unspecified, typically something human or at least animate. The first option is illustrated in (52b) and (53b), where *PRO* is necessarily bound by the main clause subject *they* (*ellos*). The second option is illustrated in (54), where *PRO* is the subject of the infinitival clause that is part of the subject NP, as indicated by the brackets:

(54)
[NP El [C *PRO* viajar en tren]] es agradable.
[NP The [C *PRO* to-travel by train]] is pleasant.
"Traveling by train is pleasant."

The limitation to animate entities in this unspecified interpretation is illustrated in such sentences as (5.5), where we may understand the sentence to mean that it is

Thus as the meaning indicates, *happy* does not actually modify the overt subject *they* in (52b).

unusual for a person to fall to the ground but not that it is unusual for a rock to fall to the ground:

(55)

To fall to the ground is unusual.

The same is true in other languages, as in the corresponding Spanish example *Caer al suelo no es común* ("To fall to the ground is not common").

In its semantic function *PRO* is in part similar to pronouns, in part similar to anaphors such as the reflexive. Like a reflexive and unlike a pronoun, it is necessarily bound if an antecedent is available, as in (52b) and (53b), where it is impossible to understand the sentence with the unspecified interpretation of *PRO* that we find in (54) and (55). Like a pronoun but unlike a reflexive, *PRO* may be free if no antecedent is available. (In fact, something similar is true of the Spanish reflexive clitic *se,* which can have an unspecified interpretation with no antecedent, as in *Se habla inglés aquí* ("One speaks English here," "English is spoken here"), but this is not generally true of reflexives in other languages, and the situation in this case is more complex.) *PRO* is also unlike overt pronouns and *pro* in that it does not require case and may therefore appear as the subject of an infinitive—and indeed, is limited to such positions. Presumably, these properties are all related, but how is not clearly understood.

We can return now to the construction (28):

(28)

Juan cree estar enfermo.

Juan believes to be sick.

As we saw earlier, this sentence is not derived by raising, leaving a trace as subject of *estar*. Evidently, the structure of (28) is

(56)

Juan cree [PRO estar enfermo].
Juan believes [PRO to be sick].

Here *Juan* and *PRO* each constitute a single-membered chain. Each of these has its separate semantic role, and *Juan* but not *PRO* has case, as required. Because an antecedent for *PRO* is available, namely *Juan, PRO* must be understood as bound by *Juan*, not with the unspecified interpretation (that is, meaning "Juan believes someone or other to be sick"), as in the case just discussed.

Notice that English lacks such constructions as (28); that is, (56) is not a possible construction in English. The element *PRO* can appear in English as the subject of an infinitive, as we have seen, but not in such constructions as (56). To express the contents of (28), English would have to use the expression

(57)

John believes [himself to be sick].

Recall that this construction is permitted in English, alongside of others, such as

(58)

a. John believes [Bill to be intelligent].
b. John expects [Bill to win the race].
c. John caused [the book to fall to the floor].

Constructions such as (57) and (58) are permitted in English because English has a device that permits the main verb to assign its accusative case to the subject of the embedded infinitival clause; lacking this device, Spanish does not admit these expressions. The same distinction between English and Spanish in fact bars *PRO* from the infinitival subject position in English while permitting it in Spanish; quite typically, *PRO* does not appear in positions to which case is assigned. There is a good bit more to say about these topics, but this would take us into new areas that I cannot explore here.

The different properties of *pro* and *PRO* have a variety of consequences. Consider the sentences

(59)
a. El que [llueva] es agradable.
   The that [rains] is pleasant.
   "It is pleasant that it rains."
b. El [llover] es agradable.
   The [to rain] is pleasant.
   "It is pleasant for it to rain."

The first is acceptable, the second is not (English has no precisely analogous expressions, lacking any similar device to form noun phrases from clauses). The finite clause demarcated by brackets in (59a) has *pro* as subject; the infinitival clause demarcated by brackets in (59b) (compare (54)) has *PRO* as its subject. Thus the structures of these clauses are (60a) and (60b), respectively:

(60)
a. *pro* llueva.
   pro rains.
b. *PRO* llover.
   PRO to rain.

The form (60a) is acceptable in (59a) and in isolation; the corresponding form in French or English would use an overt pronoun: *Il pleut, It is raining*. But *PRO* can receive no interpretation in (60b). It has no antecedent, and it cannot refer to an unspecified person (or animate entity) in this construction. Therefore the construction is impossible. Correspondingly, the English translation of (59b) can be "It is pleasant for it to rain," but not "It is pleasant to rain" with the structure "It is pleasant [*PRO* to rain]." Since the *for-to* infinitivals of English do not have a Spanish counterpart, the thought cannot be expressed in Spanish with an infinitival construction.

The difference between *pro* and *PRO* is also illustrated in sentences involving verbs such as *pedir,* which take a subject, an object, and a complement clause, which as usual can be finite or infinitival:[5]

(61)
a. María le pidió a Juan que [hablara con los muchachos].
María him-asked to Juan that [he/she-speak with the boys].
"María requested of Juan that [he/she speak to the boys]."
b. María le pidió a Juan [hablar con los muchachos].
María him-asked to Juan [to-speak with the boys].
"María asked Juan to speak to the boys."

In (61a) the subject of *hablara* ("speak") can be understood to be *María, Juan,* or in fact someone else, as determined by the discourse situation. The reason is that the subject of *hablara* in the mental representation is *pro,* which is a normal pronoun (except that it is not pronounced); and a pronoun can have the range of referential possibilities just illustrated. But sentence (61b) in Spanish has a single interpretation: *María* must be understood as the subject of *hablar.* Here the subject of *hablar* in the mental representation is *PRO,* and it is a semantic property of the verb *pedir* that the *PRO* subject of its complement must be bound by the subject of *pedir,* rather as in the English construction "María asked permission of Juan

---

5. Note that the *le-a Juan* construction is rather similar to the discontinuous *lo-él* pronominal construction illustrated in earlier examples; in all these cases Spanish has a clitic pronoun attached to the verb associated with the direct (or in this case indirect) object of the verb.

to speak to the boys," where *María* must be the subject of *speak*. Note that the situation in English is different. Here, *Juan* would normally be taken as the subject of *speak*, that is, the antecedent of the *PRO* subject of *speak*, in (61b). The verbs *pedir* and *ask* are thus slightly different in their syntactic-semantic properties.

Suppose that instead of (61) we have the sentences

(62)
a. Juan les pidió a los compañeros que [estuvieran callados].
   Juan them-asked to the pals that [they-be quiet].
   "Juan asked his pals that they be quiet."
b. Juan les pidió a los compañeros [estar callados].
   Juan them-asked to the pals [to be quiet (plural)].
   "Juan asked his pals to be quiet (plural)."

In (62a) the *pro* subject of the plural verb *estuvieran* must be plural, so it is either bound by *los compañeros* or free, referring to some individuals otherwise identified. *Juan* is not a possible antecedent in this case because of disagreement in number. In (62b), once again, the *PRO* subject of *estar* must be bound by the subject *Juan* of the main clause. But if so, then *callados*, being plural, will not be able to modify any noun. It cannot modify the *PRO* subject of *estar*, which is singular, and it cannot modify *los compañeros*, which is outside its clause. So the sentence has no interpretation. In English, in contrast, the *PRO* subject of "to be quiet" can (and normally would) take the object "his pals" as its antecedent (and, of course, number is not indicated on the adjective). Thus, although the Spanish sentence (62b) has no interpretation, the English close counterpart has a definite interpretation.

Examples of these kinds distinguish *PRO* from *pro*. To distinguish *PRO* from trace, consider again the sentence (25):

129

(25)

Juan parece [*t* conocerlo bien a él].
Juan seems [*t* to-know-him well to him].
"Juan seems to know him well."

Here *t* is the trace of *Juan,* so that we have the chain (*Juan, t*). If we had selected the reflexive pronoun instead of the third-person discontinuous pronoun *lo-él,* we would have

(63)

Juan parece [*t* conocerse bien a sí mismo].
Juan seems [*t* to-know-himself well to himself].
"Juan seems [*t* to know himself well]."

Here the antecedent of the discontinuous form *se–sí mismo* is the trace *t,* ultimately *Juan.* Similarly, in the English translation, the antecedent of the reflexive *himself* is the trace *t,* indicated in the translation, ultimately *Juan,* the antecedent of this trace, the head of the chain (*Juan, t*) that is the abstract representation of *Juan.*

The situation is quite different if we have *PRO* rather than trace as the subject of the embedded infinitival clause. Consider the examples (64) and (65), which seem superficially similar to those with the main verb *parecer:*

(64)

Juan nos mandaba [*PRO* conocerlo mejor a él].
Juan us-asked [*PRO* to-know-him better to him].
"Juan asked us to know him better."

(65)

Juan nos mandaba [*PRO* concerse mejor a sí mismo].
Juan us-asked [*PRO* to-know-himself better to himself].
"Juan asked us to know himself better."

The first of these, (64), is a properly formed sentence; the second, (65), is not, despite the fairly close similarity to

(63), which differs in that it has trace, not *PRO,* as the subject of the embedded clause. Why is this the case?

We know that the empty category in (65) is *PRO,* not trace. The reason is that the subject of the main clause has an independent semantic role, so nothing could have moved to this position or else the chain condition stated earlier would be violated. The verb *mandar,* as distinct from *pedir,* has the lexical property that its object, not its subject, binds the *PRO* subject of its clausal complement (it is thus similar to the English *ask* in its more normal usage). The object of *mandaba* in (64) and (65) is the clitic *nos,* moved from its postverbal position to before the verb, as usual. Hence *nos* binds *PRO* in these sentences. In (64) *nos,* not *Juan,* is understood to be the subject of *conocer* because it is *nos* that binds the *PRO* subject of *conocer.* Thus the meaning of (64) is "Juan asked us that we know him better."

Turning to (65), we see again that *nos* binds *PRO,* which is the antecedent of the reflexive *se–sí mismo.* But since *PRO* is now first-person plural (being bound by *nos* ("us")), it cannot bind the third-person singular reflexive *se–sí mismo,* and sentence (65) receives no interpretation. Although (63), with trace as subject of *conocer,* is acceptable, (65), with *PRO* as subject of *conocer,* is not.

Suppose that in (65) we had the first-person plural reflexive instead of the third-person singular; thus

(66)
Juan nos mandaba [*PRO* concernos mejor a nosotros mismos].
Juan us-asked [*PRO* to-know-us better to ourselves].
"Juan asked us to know ourselves better."

Again, *PRO* is bound by the object *nos* of the main verb *mandaba,* and *PRO* is the antecedent of the discontinuous reflexive *nos–nosotros mismos* ("ourselves"). But now the sentence is acceptable, with the interpretation given.

Notice that in these examples a difference in the way semantic roles are assigned produces a difference in the way anaphors can be bound. Because *parecer* assigns no semantic role to its subject, the subject of its complement can raise to this position and it can bind a reflexive in the complement clause. But *mandar* does assign a semantic role to its subject, so that the subject of its complement clause cannot raise to this position. The subject must be *PRO* in the infinitival complement and must itself bind a reflexive that appears in this clause. Because the subject of *mandar* does not bind *PRO*, it cannot serve as the antecedent of a reflexive in the complement clause.

Throughout the discussion we find illustrations of Plato's problem, illustrations that become more complex as we proceed. The person who has mastered any human language has developed a system of knowledge that is rich and complex. This cognitive system provides specific and precise knowledge of many intricate and surprising facts. It seems that the mind carries out precise computational operations, using mental representations of a specific form, to arrive at precise conclusions about factual matters of no little complexity, without conscious thought or deliberation. The principles that determine the nature of the mental representations and the operations that apply to them form a central part of our biologically determined nature. They constitute the human language faculty, which one might regard as an "organ of the mind/brain." As inquiry reveals its often surprising properties, we become better able to approach Plato's problem and to solve it and also to understand, in part at least, how we are capable of using language in normal life in the manner that we do, though Descartes's problem, the problem posed by the creative aspect of language use, still remains to be addressed. I turn to this and other questions that lie on (or beyond) the horizon in the next chapter.

The View Beyond:
Prospects for the Study of Mind

I began these lectures by posing four central questions that arise in the study of language:

1. What do we know when we are able to speak and understand a language?
2. How is this knowledge acquired?
3. How do we use this knowledge?
4. What are the physical mechanisms involved in the representation, acquisition, and use of this knowledge?

The first question is logically prior to the others. We can proceed with the investigation of questions 2, 3, and 4 to the extent that we have some understanding of the answer to question 1.

The task of answering question 1 is basically descriptive: In pursuing it, we attempt to construct a grammar, a theory of a particular language that describes how this language assigns specific mental representations to each linguistic expression, determining its form and meaning. The second and much harder task carries us beyond, to the level of genuine explanation. In pursuing it, we attempt to construct a theory of universal grammar, a theory of the fixed and invariant principles that constitute the human language faculty and the parameters of variation associated with them. We can then, in effect, deduce particular languages by setting the parameters in one or another way. Furthermore, given the lexicon, which also satisfies the principles of universal grammar, and with the parameters set in a particular way, we can explain why the sentences of these languages have the form and meaning they do by deriving their structured representations from the principles of universal grammar.

Question 2 is the special case of Plato's problem that arises in the study of language. We can solve the problem to the extent that we succeed in constructing the theory of universal grammar, though other factors are also involved, for example, the mechanisms of parameter setting. Other special cases of Plato's problem, in other domains, will have to be addressed in much the same fashion.

Language learning, then, is the process of determining the values of the parameters left unspecified by universal grammar, of setting the switches that make the network function, to use the image I mentioned earlier. Beyond that, the language learner must discover the lexical items of the language and their properties. To a large extent this seems to be a problem of finding what labels are used for preexisting concepts, a conclusion that is so surprising as to seem outrageous but that appears to be essentially correct nevertheless.

Language learning is not really something that the child does; it is something that happens to the child placed in an appropriate environment, much as the child's body grows and matures in a predetermined way when provided with appropriate nutrition and environmental stimulation. This is not to say that the nature of the environment is irrelevant. The environment determines the way the parameters of universal grammar are set, yielding different languages. In a somewhat similar way the early visual environment determines the density of receptors for horizontal and vertical lines, as has been shown experimentally. Furthermore, the difference between a rich and stimulating environment and an impoverished environment may be substantial, in language acquisition as in physical growth or, more accurately, as in other aspects of physical growth, the acquisition of language being simply one of these aspects. Capacities that are part of our common human endowment can flourish or can be restricted and suppressed, depending on the conditions provided for their growth.

The point is probably more general. It is a traditional insight, which merits more attention than it receives, that teaching should not be compared to filling a bottle with water but rather to helping a flower to grow in its own way. As any good teacher knows, the methods of instruction and the range of material covered are matters of small importance as compared with the success in arousing the natural curiosity of the students and stimulating their interest in exploring on their own. What the student learns passively will be quickly forgotten. What students discover for themselves when their natural curiosity and creative impulses are aroused not only will be remembered but will be the basis for further exploration and inquiry and perhaps significant intellectual contributions. The same is true in connection with questions that I have been addressing in the concurrent series of lectures on social and political issues (see preface). A truly democratic community is one in which the general public has the opportunity for meaningful and constructive participation in the formation of social policy: in their own immediate community, in the workplace, and in the society at large. A society that excludes large areas of crucial decision-making from public control, or a system of governance that merely grants the general public the opportunity to ratify decisions taken by the elite groups that dominate the private society and the state, hardly merits the term "democracy."

Question 3 has two aspects: the perception aspect

and the production aspect. Thus we would like to know how people who have acquired a language put their knowledge to use in understanding what they hear and in expressing their thoughts. I have touched on the perception aspect of the question in these lectures. But I have said nothing so far about the production aspect, what I called Descartes's problem, the problem posed by the creative aspect of language use, a normal and commonplace but quite remarkable phenomenon. For a person to understand a linguistic expression, the mind/brain must determine its phonetic form and its words and then use the principles of universal grammar and the values of the parameters to project a structured representation of this expression and determine how its parts are associated. I have given a number of examples to illustrate how this process might take place. Descartes's problem, however, raises other issues that lie beyond anything we have discussed.

As for question 4, I have said nothing. Inquiry into this problem is largely a task for the future. Part of the problem in undertaking such inquiry is that experiments with human subjects are excluded for ethical reasons. We do not tolerate experimental study of humans in the manner regarded as legitimate (rightly or wrongly) in the case of animal subjects. Thus children are not raised in controlled environments to see what kind of language would develop under various experimentally devised conditions. We do not permit researchers to implant electrodes in the human brain to investigate its internal operations or to remove parts of the brain surgically to determine what the effects would be, as is done routinely in the case of nonhuman subjects. Researchers are restricted to "nature's experiments": injury, disease, and so on. To attempt to discover brain mechanisms under these conditions is extremely difficult.

In the case of other systems of the mind/brain, the

human visual system, for example, the experimental study of other organisms (cats, monkeys, etc.) is highly informative because the visual systems are apparently quite similar among these species. But as far as we know, the language faculty is a distinctive human possession. Study of the brain mechanisms of other animals tells us little if anything about this faculty of the mind/brain.

The answers to these four questions that we would be inclined to give today (or at least, that we *should* be inclined to give today, in my view) are quite different from those that were accepted with little controversy as recently as a generation ago. To the extent that these questions were even posed, the answers offered would then have been something like the following. Language is a habit system, a system of dispositions to behavior, acquired through training and conditioning. Any innovative aspects of this behavior are the result of "analogy." The physical mechanisms are essentially those involved in catching a ball and other skilled performances. Plato's problem was unrecognized or dismissed as trivial. It was generally believed that language is "overlearned"; the problem is to account for the fact that so much experience and training are needed to establish such simple skills. As for Descartes's problem, it too was unrecognized within academic circles, the applied disciplines, and the intellectual community at large.

Attention to the facts quickly demonstrates that these ideas are not simply in error but entirely beyond any hope of repair. They must be abandoned, as essentially worthless. One has to turn to the domain of ideology to find comparable instances of a collection of ideas accepted so widely and with so little question, and so utterly divorced from the real world. And, in fact, that is the direction in which we should turn if we are interested in finding out how and why these myths achieved the respectability accorded to them, how they came to dominate such a large part of intellectual life and discourse. That is an interesting topic, one well worth pursuing, but I will not undertake this project here, apart from a few comments later on. If we were to pursue it, we would, I think, find ourselves in the domain of the second series of lectures that I have been giving here in Managua (see preface). Let us return to Descartes's problem, the problem of how language is used in the normal creative fashion, as I described earlier. Notice that I am not concerned here with use of language that has true aesthetic value, with what we call true creativity, as in the work of a fine poet or novelist or an exceptional stylist. Rather, what I have in mind is something more mundane: the ordinary use of language in everyday life, with its distinctive properties of novelty, freedom from control by external stimuli and inner states, coherence and appropriateness to situations, and its capacity to evoke appropriate thoughts in the listener. The history of this problem is of some interest.

The issue arose in the context of the mind-body problem or, more specifically, what was later called "the problem of other minds." Descartes developed a mechanical theory of the universe, a major contribution to the physical sciences of his day. He convinced himself that virtually everything that takes place in the universe of our experience can be explained in terms of his mechanical conceptions, in terms of bodies that interact through direct contact—a "contact mechanics" we might call it. In these terms he sought to explain everything from the motion of the heavenly bodies to the behavior of animals and much of the behavior and perception of humans as well. He apparently felt that he had largely succeeded in this task and that all that remained was to fill in the details in his overarching conceptions. But not all our experience could be accommodated within this framework. The most striking exception, he suggested, was what I called earlier the creative aspect of language use. This falls entirely beyond the conceptions of mechanics, so Descartes argued.

Through introspection each person can perceive that he or she has a mind, which is quite distinct in its properties from the bodies that constitute the physical world. Suppose now that I want to determine whether another creature also has a mind. The Cartesians proposed that in this case, one should undertake a certain experimental program, designed to determine whether this organism exhibits distinctive features of human behavior, the creative aspect of language use being the most striking example and the one most readily investigated. If the organs of a parrot are placed in a certain configuration under given stimulus conditions, the Cartesians argued, what the parrot "says" is strictly determined (or it may be random). But this is not true of an organism with a mind like ours, and experiment should be able to reveal this fact. Many specific tests were proposed. If these tests convince us that the organism exhibits the creative aspect of language use, then it would be unreasonable to doubt that it has a mind like ours.

More generally, as I mentioned earlier, the problem is that a "machine" is compelled to act in a certain way under fixed environmental conditions and with its parts arranged in a certain way, while a human under these circumstances is only "incited and inclined" to behave in this fashion. The human may often, or even always, do what it is incited or inclined to do, but each of us knows from introspection that we have a choice in the matter over a large range. And we can determine by experiment that this is true of other humans as well. The difference between being *compelled,* and merely being *incited and inclined,* is a crucial one, the Cartesians concluded—and quite accurately. The distinction would remain crucial even if it were not manifested in actual behavior. If it were not, one could give an accurate description of human behavior in mechanical terms, but it would not be a true characterization of essential features of the human being and of the sources of human behavior. To account for the facts about the world that surpass the possibilities of mechanical explanation, it is necessary to find some extramechanical principle, what we might call a creative principle. This principle, the Cartesians argued, belongs to mind, a "second substance" entirely separate from body, which is subject to mechanical explanation. Descartes himself wrote a lengthy treatise in which he laid out the principles of the mechanical world. It was to include a final volume devoted to the mind, but allegedly Descartes destroyed this part of his comprehensive work when he learned of the fate of Galileo before the Inquisition, which compelled him to renounce his beliefs about the physical world. In his preserved writings Descartes suggests that we may not "have intelligence enough" to discover the nature of mind, although "we are so conscious of the liberty and indifference [absence of strict determination] which exists in us that there is nothing that we comprehend more clearly and perfectly," and "it would be absurd to doubt that of which we inwardly experience and perceive as existing within ourselves just because we do not comprehend a matter which from its nature we know to be incomprehensible."

For the Cartesians, mind is a single substance, distinct from body. Much of the speculation and debate of the period dealt with the question of how these two substances interact—how the decisions of the mind might lead to actions of the body, for example. There is no such thing as an "animal mind" because animals are merely machines, subject to mechanical explanation. There is no possibility in this conception of a *human mind* as distinct from other kinds of mind, or of differently constituted human minds. A creature is either human or it is not; there are no "degrees of humanness," no essential variation among humans apart from superficial physical aspects. As the philosopher Harry Bracken has pointed out, racism or sexism is a logical impossibility under this dualist conception. The mind, Descartes held, is a "universal instrument which can serve for all contingencies." Notice that this claim is not consistent with his belief that we may not have intelligence enough to discover the nature of mind. The conclusion that the mind has intrinsic limits is surely the correct one; the idea that it is a "universal instrument" might be regarded as one of the ancestors of the widely held belief that the human language faculty, and other cognitive systems, all fall within the bounds of "general learning mechanisms" that are applicable to every intellectual task.

The Cartesian tests for the existence of other minds have been resurrected in a new guise in recent years, most notably by the British mathematician Alan Turing, who devised what is now called the Turing test, to determine whether a machine (for example, a programmed computer) exhibits intelligent behavior. We apply the Turing test to a device by submitting to it a series of questions and asking whether its responses can deceive a human observer who will conclude that the responses are being offered by another human being. In Cartesian terms this would be a test of whether the device has a mind like ours.

How should we respond today to these ideas? Descartes's argument is far from absurd and cannot easily be discounted. If indeed the principles of mechanics do not suffice to explain certain phenomena, then we must appeal to something beyond these principles to explain them. So far, that is familiar science. We need not accept the Cartesian metaphysics, which required postulation of a "second substance," a "thinking substance" (*res cogi-*

142

tans), undifferentiated, without components or interacting subparts, the seat of consciousness that accounts for the "unity of consciousness" and the immortality of the soul. All of this is entirely unsatisfying and provides no real answer to any of the problems raised. The problems themselves, however, are quite serious ones, and much as Descartes held, it would be absurd to deny the facts that are apparent to us merely because we can conceive of no way of solving them.

It is interesting to observe the fate of the Cartesian version of the mind-body problem and the problem of the existence of other minds. The mind-body problem can be posed sensibly only insofar as we have a definite conception of body. If we have no such definite and fixed conception, we cannot ask whether some phenomena fall beyond its range. The Cartesians offered a fairly definite conception of body in terms of their contact mechanics, which in many respects reflects commonsense understanding. Therefore they could sensibly formulate the mind-body problem and the problem of other minds. There was important work attempting to develop the concept of mind further, including studies by British Neoplatonists of the seventeenth century that explored the categories and principles of perception and cognition along lines that were later extended by Kant and that were rediscovered, independently, in twentieth-century gestalt psychology.

Another line of development was the "general and philosophical grammar" (in our terms, scientific grammar) of the seventeenth, eighteenth, and early nineteenth centuries, which was much influenced by Cartesian conceptions, particularly in the early period. These inquiries into universal grammar sought to lay bare the general principles of language. These were regarded as not essentially different from the general principles of thought, so that language is "a mirror of mind," in the conventional phrase. For various reasons—some good, some not—

these inquiries were disparaged and abandoned for a century, to be resurrected, again independently, a generation ago, though in quite different terms and without recourse to any dualist assumptions.

It is also interesting to see how the Cartesian conception of body and mind entered social thought, most strikingly in the libertarian ideas of Jean-Jacques Rousseau, which were based on strictly Cartesian conceptions of body and mind. Because humans, possessing minds, are crucially distinct from machines (including animals), so Rousseau argued, and because the properties of mind crucially surpass mechanical determinacy, therefore any infringement on human freedom is illegitimate and must be confronted and overcome. Although the later development of such thinking abandoned the Cartesian framework, its origins lie in significant measure in these classical ideas.

The Cartesian conception of a second substance was generally abandoned in later years, but it is important to recognize that it was not the theory of mind that was refuted (one might argue that it was hardly clear enough to be confirmed or refuted). Rather, the Cartesian concept of *body* was refuted by seventeenth-century physics, particularly in the work of Isaac Newton, which laid the foundations for modern science. Newton demonstrated that the motions of the heavenly bodies could not be explained by the principles of Descartes's contact mechanics, so that the Cartesian concept of body must be abandoned. In the Newtonian framework there is a "force" that one body exerts on another, without contact between them, a kind of "action at a distance." Whatever this force may be, it does not fall within the Cartesian framework of contact mechanics. Newton himself found this conclusion unsatisfying. He sometimes referred to gravitational force as "occult" and suggested that his theory gave only a mathematical description of events in the physical world, not a true "philosophical" (in more modern terminology, "scientific") explanation of these events. Until the late nineteenth century it was still widely held that a true explanation must be framed somehow in mechanical or quasi-mechanical terms. Others, notably the chemist and philosopher Joseph Priestley, argued that bodies themselves possess capacities that go beyond the limits of contact mechanics, specifically the property of attracting other bodies, but perhaps far more. Without pursuing subsequent developments further, the general conclusion is that the Cartesian concept of body was found to be untenable.

What is the concept of body that finally emerged? The answer is that there is no clear and definite concept of body. If the best theory of the material world that we can construct includes a variety of forces, particles that have no mass, and other entities that would have been offensive to the "scientific common sense" of the Cartesians, then so be it: We conclude that these are properties of the physical world, the world of body. The conclusions are tentative, as befits empirical hypotheses, but are not subject to criticism because they transcend some a priori conception of body. There is no longer any definite conception of body. Rather, the material world is whatever we discover it to be, with whatever properties it must be assumed to have for the purposes of explanatory theory. Any intelligible theory that offers genuine explanations and that can be assimilated to the core notions of physics becomes part of the theory of the material world, part of our account of body. If we have such a theory in some domain, we seek to assimilate it to the core notions of physics, perhaps modifying these notions as we carry out this enterprise. In the study of human psychology, if we develop a theory of some cognitive faculty (the language faculty, for example) and find that this faculty has certain properties, we seek to discover the mechanisms of the brain that exhibit these properties and to account for them in the terms of the physical sciences—keeping open the possibility that the concepts of the physical sciences might have to be modified, just as the concepts of Cartesian contact mechanics had to be modified to account for the motion of the heavenly bodies, and as has happened repeatedly in the evolution of the natural sciences since Newton's day.

In short, there is no definite concept of body. Rather, there is a material world, the properties of which are to be discovered, with no a priori demarcation of what will count as "body." The mind-body problem can therefore not even be formulated. The problem cannot be solved, because there is no clear way to state it. Unless someone proposes a definite concept of body, we cannot ask whether some phenomena exceed its bounds. Similarly, we cannot pose the problem of other minds. We can, and I think should, continue to use mentalistic terminology, as I have done throughout in discussing mental representations and operations that form and modify them in mental computation. But we do not see ourselves as investigating the properties of some "second substance," something crucially distinct from body that interacts with body in some mysterious way, perhaps through divine intervention. Rather, we are studying the properties of the material world at a level of abstraction at which we believe, rightly or wrongly, that a genuine explanatory theory can be constructed, a theory that provides genuine insight into the nature of the phenomena that concern us. These phenomena, in fact, are of real intellectual interest not so much in themselves but in the avenue that they provide for us to penetrate into the deeper workings of the mind. Ultimately, we hope to assimilate this study to the mainstream of the natural sciences, much as the study of genes or of valence and the properties of the chemical elements was assimilated to more fundamental sciences.

We recognize, however, that, as in the past, it may turn out that these fundamental sciences must be modified or extended to provide foundations for the abstract theories of complex systems, such as the human mind.

Our task, then, is to discover genuine explanatory theories and to use these discoveries to facilitate inquiry into physical mechanisms with the properties outlined in these theories. Wherever this inquiry leads, it will be within the domain of "body." Or more accurately, we simply abandon the whole conception of body as possibly distinct from something else and use the methods of rational inquiry to learn as much as we can about the world—what we call the material world, whatever exotic properties it turns out to have.

The mind-body problem remains the subject of much controversy, debate, and speculation, and in this regard the problem is still very much alive. But the discussion seems to me incoherent in fundamental respects. Unlike the Cartesians, we have no definite concept of body. It is therefore quite unclear how we can even ask whether some phenomena lie beyond the range of the study of body, falling within the separate study of mind.

Recall the logic of Descartes's argument for the existence of a second substance, *res cogitans*. Having defined "body" in terms of contact mechanics, he argued that certain phenomena lie beyond its domain, so that some new principle was required; given his metaphysics, a second substance must be postulated. The logic is essentially sound; it is, in fact, much like Newton's, when he demonstrated the inadequacy of Cartesian contact mechanics for the explanation of the motion of the heavenly bodies so that a new principle, the principle of gravitational attraction, had to be postulated. The crucial difference between the Cartesian and the Newtonian enterprises was that the latter offered a genuine explanatory theory of the behavior of bodies, whereas the Cartesian theory offered no satisfactory account of properties such the creative aspect of language use that lie beyond mechanical explanation in Descartes's view. Therefore Newton's conceptions came to be the "scientific common sense" of later generations of scientists, while Descartes's fell by the wayside.

Returning now to Descartes's problem, notice that it still stands, unresolved by these developments in the natural sciences. We still have no way to come to terms with what appears to be a fact, even an obvious fact: Our actions are free and undetermined, in that we need not do what we are "incited and inclined" to do; and if we do what we are incited and inclined to do, an element of free choice nevertheless enters. Despite much thought and often penetrating analysis, it seems to me that this problem still remains unsolved, much in the way Descartes formulated it. Why should this be so?

One possibility, of course, is that no one has yet thought of the right idea that will yield a solution to the problem. That is possible, but it is not the only possibility. Another possibility is the one suggested by Descartes: The problem escapes our intellectual grasp.

When we investigate other organisms, we discover that their capacities have a certain scope and certain limits. Thus a rat can do certain things very well. Suppose that we construct a radial maze, an experimental design consisting of a center with straight paths leading from it much like the spokes of a wheel. Suppose that at the end of each path there is a container with a single pellet of food. A rat placed in the center can quickly learn to obtain the food with maximal efficiency, running through each path only once. This remains true even if the device is rotated, leaving the food containers fixed, so that the rate has to traverse the same physical path more than once. This is no mean accomplishment; it requires rather sophisticated spatial concepts. On the other hand, rats apparently cannot learn to run mazes that involve sequential concepts (for example, turn right twice, then turn left twice). Surely, no rat could learn to run a maze that required turning right at every choice point corresponding to a prime number, left elsewhere: thus turn right at the second, third, fifth, seventh, eleventh, etc., choice point. A human could presumably solve this problem, though not without difficulty and not without conscious knowledge of arithmetic. Putting particular examples aside, it is obvious that the rat (pigeon, monkey, etc.) has fixed capacities, with a definite scope and definite limits.

The point is a logical one. If a creature has the capacity to perform certain tasks well, then these very capacities will lead to failure in some other tasks. If we can learn what these capacities are, we can design problems that the creature will be unable to solve, because they fall beyond its capacities. A creature is fortunate if there are problems that it cannot solve, because this means that it has the capacity to solve certain other problems well. The distinction may be one of ease or difficulty, or it may be one of possibility versus literal impossibility. But the distinction must exist, as a matter of logic. The nature of the distinction is a matter of fact; the existence of such distinctions cannot be in doubt.

Furthermore, a problem that is readily solved by one organism may be too difficult or impossible for another. We can, for example, easily design a device that will solve the "prime number maze" and do so instantaneously and without effort or trials, namely, by building the answer into the mechanisms themselves. But this device will not be able to solve what we regard as much simpler mazes. Organisms are not arrayed along a spectrum, with some "more intelligent" than others, simply capable of solving more complex problems. Rather, they differ in the array of problems that they are capable of addressing and solving. A certain species of wasp, or a pigeon, is designed to find its way home; a human is not designed in the same way and cannot perform similar tasks readily or at all. It is not that a wasp or pigeon is "more intelligent" than a human; rather, it is different in its biologically determined capacities. Furthermore, there is no clear "absolute sense" in which problems are simple or difficult. It may be possible to formulate an "absolute notion" of difficulty that is useful for certain purposes in terms of the mathematical theory of computation. But it is not clear that this notion would be of much interest for psychology or biology, at least in the present context, because what is important for the behavior of an organism is its special design and the array of "difficulty" of problems that is determined by this special design.

We suppose that humans are part of the natural world. They plainly have the capacity to solve certain problems. It follows that they lack the capacity to solve other problems, which will either be far too difficult for them to handle within existing limitations of time, memory, and so on or will literally be beyond the scope of their intelligence in principle. The human mind cannot be in Descartes's terms a "universal instrument which can serve for all contingencies." That is fortunate, for if it were such a universal instrument, it would serve equally badly for all contingencies. We could deal with no problems at all with any measure of success.

In the case of language the language faculty, a physical mechanism in the sense already explained, has certain definite properties, not others. These are the properties that the theory of universal grammar seeks to formulate and describe. These properties permit the human mind to acquire a language of a specific type, with curious and surprising features, as we have seen. The same properties exclude other possible languages as "unlearnable" by the language faculty. Possibly a human could come to understand such a nonhuman language by using other faculties of the mind, much in the manner in which humans can come to understand many things about the nature of the physical world through an arduous process of controlled inquiry and experimentation extending over many generations and with the intervention of individual genius (whatever that may be). Other such languages would be beyond the bounds of possible human thought. To the extent that we can discover the properties of the language faculty, we can construct "unlearnable languages," languages that cannot be acquired by the language faculty because at every point it will make the wrong choices, the wrong guesses as to the nature of the language. To the extent that we can discover the properties of other faculties of the mind, we can construct languages that can be acquried only with great difficulty, in the manner of scientific inquiry, or, presumably, not at all, and we can design other tasks that are extremely difficult or insoluble (for human intelligence).

There is nothing particularly mysterious about all of this. Much of what I have just said is a matter of logic. The specific scope and limits of the various faculties of the human mind are matters of fact, matters in principle amenable to human inquiry, unless they transcend the limits of the human mind. We might, someday, even be able to discover that the human mind is so constructed that certain problems, which we can formulate, are beyond the possibility of solution by a human intelligence. Such problems might be quite "simple" for an intelligence differently constructed, just as the prime number maze would have an obvious solution for a device designed to solve this problem.

All of this is transparent in the study of physical growth. Humans are designed to grow arms and legs, not wings. Lacking appropriate nutrition or in an environment that is deficient in other ways, the embryo may fail to grow arms and legs properly, but no change in the environment will lead it to grow wings. If physical growth merely reflected properties of the environment, we would be shapeless, formless creatures, unlike one another, with extremely limited physical capacities. Since our biological endowment is intricate and highly specific, the way we grow does not reflect properties of the physical environment but rather our essential nature. We therefore grow to be complex organisms with quite specific physical properties, very similar to one another in our basic properties, adapted to certain tasks but not to others—walking but not flying, for example. The environment is not irrelevant to growth. Rather, growth is triggered by the environment in numerous ways, stimulated by environmental factors or retarded or distorted if the requisite factors are lacking. But it takes place largely in predetermined ways. We are lucky that we are incapable of becoming birds, because this follows from the fact that we are capable of becoming humans.

There is every reason to suppose that much the same is true of mental development. Indeed, this must be so if we are truly part of the physical world. It follows that we can readily deal with certain problems—learning of human language, for example—while others, which are neither "harder" nor "easier" in any useful absolute terms, are beyond our reach, some of them forever. We are fortunate that this is so.

Let us return again to Descartes's problem. One possible reason for the lack of success in solving it or even presenting sensible ideas about it is that it is not within the range of human intellectual capacities: It is either "too difficult," given the nature of our capacities, or beyond their limits altogether. There is some reason to suspect that this may be so, though we do not know enough about human intelligence or the properties of the problem to be sure. We are able to devise theories to deal with strict determinacy and with randomness. But these concepts do not seem appropriate to Descartes's problem, and it may be that the relevant concepts are not accessible to us. A Martian scientist, with a mind different from ours, might regard this problem as trivial, and wonder why humans never seem to hit on the obvious way of solving it. This observer might also be amazed at the ability of every human child to acquire language, something that seems to him incomprehensible, requiring divine intervention, because the elements of the language faculty lie beyond his conceptual range.

The same is true of the arts. Work of true aesthetic value follows canons and principles that are only in part subject to human choice; in part, they reflect our fundamental nature. The result is that we can experience deep emotion—pleasure, pain, excitement, and so on—from certain creative work, though how and why remains largely unknown. But the very capacities of mind that open these possibilities to us exclude other possibilities, some forever. The limits of artistic creativity should, again, be a matter of joy, not sorrow, because they follow from the fact that there is a rich domain of aesthetic experience to which we have access.

The same is true of moral judgment. What its basis may be we do not know, but we can hardly doubt that it is rooted in fundamental human nature. It cannot be merely a matter of convention that we find some things to be right, others wrong. Growing up in a particular society, a child acquires standards and principles of moral judgment. These are acquired on the basis of limited evidence, but they have broad and often quite precise applicability. It is often though not always true that people can discover or be convinced that their judgments about a particular case are wrong, in the sense that the judgments are inconsistent with the person's own internalized principles. Moral argument is not always pointless, merely a matter of "I assert this" and "you assert that." The acquisition of a specific moral and ethical system, wide ranging and often precise in its consequences, cannot simply be the result of "shaping" and "control" by the social environment. As in the case of language, the environment is far too impoverished and indeterminate to provide this system to the child, in its full richness and applicability. Knowing little about the matter, we are compelled to speculate; but it certainly seems reasonable to speculate that the moral and ethical system acquired by the child owes much to some innate human faculty. The environment is relevant, as in the case of language, vision, and so on; thus we can find individual and cultural divergence. But there is surely a common basis, rooted in our nature.

The course of our own civilization may offer some insight into the matter. Not long ago, slavery was considered legitimate, even estimable; slave owners did not characteristically regard what they were doing as wrong but rather saw it as a proof of their high moral values. Their arguments were, furthermore, not absurd, though we now regard them as morally grotesque. Thus, in the early days of industrial capitalism, slave owners could—and did—point out that if you own a piece of machinery, you are likely to treat it with more care than if you merely rent it. Similarly, the slave owner is likely to treat his possession with more care and solicitude than the capitalist who merely rents people for his temporary purposes. Slavery, then, reflects higher moral standards than "wage slavery." No sane person would now accept this argument, though it is not entirely absurd by any means. As civilization progressed, it came to be understood that slavery is an infringement on essential human rights. We may look forward to the day when wage slavery and the need to rent oneself to survive may be seen in a similar light, as we come to have better understanding of the moral values rooted in our inner nature.

Many of us have experienced something similar during our own lifetimes. Not many years ago the problems of sexism were barely on the agenda. They are far from overcome, but they are at least recognized, and it is widely understood that they must be addressed. This is a change of moral consciousness, probably irrevocable, like the realization that slavery is an intolerable affront to human dignity. It is not merely a change but an advance, an advance toward understanding of our own nature and the moral and ethical principles that derive from it.

There may be no end to such discoveries, if civilization survives. A truly decent and honest person will always seek to discover forms of oppression, hierarchy, domination, and authority that infringe fundamental human rights. As some are overcome, others will be revealed that previously were not part of our conscious awareness. We thus come to a better understanding of who and what we are in our inner nature, and who and what we should be in our actual lives.

This is an optimistic view, and it would not be difficult to bring forth historical evidence that apparently refutes it, but perhaps it is not unrealistic to adopt this perspective in thinking about our history and the prospects for what lies ahead. Moral thought and discourse may not end with such considerations as these. But such considerations should, nevertheless, inform and enrich it.

I mentioned that Rousseau derived libertarian conceptions from Cartesian principles of body and mind. These ideas were developed further in French and German Romanticism, still framed within assumptions about essential human nature. In the libertarian social theory of Wilhelm von Humboldt, who greatly influenced John Stuart Mill (and was also, incidentally, a major figure in linguistics whose ideas are only now coming to be appreciated), it is an essential human right, rooted in the "human essence," to be able to carry out productive and creative work under one's own control in solidarity with others. If a person creates some beautiful object under external direction and control, Humboldt argued, we may admire what he does, but we despise what he is—a machine, not a full human being. Marx's theory of alienated labor, the basis of his social thought, developed from these grounds, and in his early work he too formulated these conceptions in terms of a "species property" that determines certain fundamental human rights: crucially, the right of workers to control production, its nature and conditions. Bakunin argued that humans have "an instinct of freedom" and that infringement on this essential feature of human nature is illegitimate. The tradition of libertarian socialism developed in much these terms. Its conceptions have yet to be realized except in the most limited ways in existing societies, but in my view, at least, they are essentially correct and capture crucial features of essential human nature and the moral code that should be brought to conscious awareness, reflecting these properties.

We might observe that every form of engagement in social life is based on assumptions about human nature, usually only implicit. Adam Smith held that humans are born "to truck and barter" and, on the basis of this and similar assumptions, developed his justification for free market capitalism. The line of thought I have just briefly indicated was based on very different concepts of human nature. In ordinary everyday life the same is true. Suppose that a person decides to accept the status quo, or to try to change it, whether by reform or revolution. If not based simply on fear, greed, or other forms of abdication of moral responsibility, the decision is taken in a specific way on the basis of beliefs—explicit or implicit—about what is good and right for human beings, hence ultimately on assumptions about fundamental human nature. It could hardly be otherwise. There is, then, a truth about the matter to be discovered, and it is an intellectually challenging task, and in this case one with profound human implications, to discover the truth about the matter.

Still remaining within the realm of speculation, let us return to the study of human cognition in domains that may be more accessible to scientific inquiry. As intellectual history shows, scientists have been able over time to construct a theoretical edifice of remarkable depth in certain areas while other questions remain in much the state they were when raised millennia ago. Why should this be so? There might be some value in approaching this matter along the lines of our schematic account of language acquisition. Recalling the essentials, a child endowed with the human language faculty is presented with certain data and constructs a language, using the data to set the parameters of the language faculty. The language then provides specific interpretations for linguistic expressions over an unbounded range.

Suppose that we think of theory construction in similar terms. As part of the human biological endowment, the scientist is endowed with a certain conceptual apparatus, certain ways of formulating problems, a concept of intelligibility and explanation, and so on. Call this the science-forming capacity. As in other cases it may contain hidden resources that come to be recognized and used as the contingencies of life and experience permit, so access to this endowment may change over time. But we may assume it to be fixed, in the manner of the language faculty. The science-forming capacity is supplemented with certain background assumptions, determined by the state of current scientific understanding. So supplemented, the science-forming capacity addresses a query posed in terms accessible to it, or it formulates a query using its own resources, not at all a trivial task; the science-forming capacity then seeks to construct a theoretical explanation that will respond to this query. Its own internal criteria will determine whether the task has been successfully accomplished. If it is, the background assumptions may change, and the science-forming capacity is now prepared to face other queries, perhaps to formulate others that it will itself proceed to address. To approach the real situation of problem solving and theory construction, we must add much more, but let us keep to this schematic account. In the case of language there is a special faculty that is a central element of the human mind. It operates quickly, in a deterministic fashion, unconsciously and beyond the limits of awareness and in a manner that is common to the species, yielding a rich and complex system of knowledge, a particular language. For problem solving and theory construction there is nothing so specific. The problems we face are too varied, and the differences among people who face them are far more striking, though it is worth emphasizing that those who share the same background assumptions can generally understand a proposed theory and evaluate it even if they did not construct it themselves and perhaps lacked whatever special abilities are involved in doing so.

In most cases the science-forming capacity, presented with a query, provides no useful response at all. Most queries are just baffling. Sometimes a small number of intelligible theories are produced. The science-forming capacity, employing its resources, may then undertake a course of experiment to evaluate them. Sometimes the theories produced may be in the neighborhood of the truth, in which case we have potential knowledge, which can be refined by experiment, working at the margins. This partial congruence between the truth about the world and what the human science-forming capacity produces at a given moment yields science. Notice that it is just blind luck if the human science-forming capacity, a particular component of the human biological endowment, happens to yield a result that conforms more or less to the truth about the world. Some have argued that this is not blind luck but rather a product of Darwinian evolution. The outstanding American philosopher Charles Sanders Peirce, who presented an account of science construction in terms similar to those just outlined, argued in this vein. His point was that through ordinary processes of natural selection our mental capacities evolved so as to be able to deal with the problems that arise in the world of experience. But this argument is not compelling. It is possible to imagine that chimpanzees have an innate fear of snakes because those who lacked this genetically determined property did not survive to reproduce, but one can hardly argue that humans have the capacity to discover quantum theory for similar reasons. The experience that shaped the course of evolution offers no hint of the problems to be faced in the sciences, and ability to solve these problems could hardly have been a factor in evolution. We cannot appeal to this *deus ex machina* to explain the convergence of our ideas and the truth about the world. Rather, it is largely a lucky accident that there is such a (partial) convergence, so it seems.

The human science-forming capacity, like other biological systems, has its scope and limits, as a matter of necessity. We can be confident that some problems will lie beyond the limits, however the science-forming capacity is supplemented by appropriate background information. Descartes's problem may be among them. At least, this would not be surprising, and there is little reason now to suspect otherwise.

One might imagine that, by investigating the history of science and by experimentation with human subjects, we might learn something about the nature of the human science-forming capacity. If so, we might also learn something about the kinds of problems that we can and cannot approach by the resources of the science-forming capacity, the methods of the sciences.

There is, incidentally, no reason to suppose that all the problems we face are best approached in these terms. Thus it is quite possible—overwhelmingly probable, one might guess—that we will always learn more about human life and human personality from novels than from scientific psychology. The science-forming capacity is only one facet of our mental endowment. We use it where we can but are not restricted to it, fortunately.

Can the study of language, conducted along the lines we have investigated, provide a useful model for other aspects of the study of human cognition? The general line of approach should be just as appropriate elsewhere, but it would be astonishing if we were to discover that the constituent elements of the language faculty enter crucially in other domains. The one other area of cognitive psychology, beyond language, that has made substantial progress in recent years is the study of vision. Here too we can ask what are the properties of the human visual faculty. As I mentioned, in this case we can also learn something about the physical mechanisms involved, because of the possibility of experimentation with other organisms with similar capacities. Here too we discover that the faculty has definite and specific properties and that some possibilities of variation are determined by visual experience—the density of horizontal and vertical receptors, for example. In this case experiment reveals that the growth of the faculty to its mature state observes *critical periods;* specific aspects of the faculty must develop within a certain time frame of general maturation or else they will not develop properly or at all. Certain kinds of visual experience are necessary to trigger development during these critical periods, patterned stimulation in early infancy, for example. The visual system is unlike the language faculty in many crucial ways; it does not yield a system of knowledge, for example, but is strictly a processing system. But there are some similarities in the way the problems can be addressed.

The human visual system observes certain principles, just as the language faculty does. One of these, recently discovered, is a certain "rigidity principle." Under a wide range of conditions the eye-brain interprets the phenomena presented to it as rigid objects in motion. Thus, if I were to have in my hands a plane figure, say in the shape of a circle, and were to present it to you perpendicular to the line of sight, you would see a circular figure. If I were to rotate it 90 degrees so that it finally disappeared, you would see a circular figure rotating. The visual information reaching your eye is consistent with the conclusion that what you saw was a plane figure shrinking and changing its shape until it becomes a line and disappears. But under a wide range of conditions, what you will "see" is a rigid plane figure rotating. The eye-brain imposes this interpretation on what it sees, because of the way it is constructed. In this case the physiology of the matter is understood to some degree as well.

To take another case, suppose that you look at a television screen with a large dot at one end. Suppose the dot disappears and another dot of the same size, shape, and color appears at the other end of the screen. If the timing and distance are properly chosen, what you will "see" is a dot moving from one position to the other, a phenomenon called apparent motion. The properties of apparent motion are quite remarkable. Thus, if a horizontal line is present in the middle of the screen and the experiment is repeated, what you will "see" under appropriate conditions is motion of the dot from one end of the screen to the other, not in a straight line but moving around the barrier. If the disappearing dot is red and the appearing one blue, you will see a red dot moving across the screen, becoming blue at a certain point and continuing to its final location. And so on, under a variety of other conditions. All these phenomena reflect the structure of the visual mechanisms.

The visual mechanisms of other organisms operate quite differently. Thus, in a series of classical experiments about twenty-five years ago, it was demonstrated that the eye of a frog is designed, in effect, to "see" a fly in motion. If there is a certain kind of motion, similar to that of a fly, the eye-brain will see it, but a dead fly placed in the line of sight will not trigger the visual mechanism and will not be seen. Here also the physiological mechanisms are known.

These principles might be regarded as in some sense comparable to the principles of the language faculty. They are, of course, entirely different principles. The language faculty does not include the rigidity principle or the principles that govern apparent motion, and the visual faculty does not include the principles of binding theory, case theory, structure dependence, and so on. The two systems operate in quite different ways, not surprisingly.

What is known about other cognitive domains suggests that the same is true elsewhere, though so little is known that one cannot be sure. It seems that the mind is *modular,* to use a technical term, consisting of separate systems with their own properties. Of course, the systems interact; we can describe what we see, hear, smell, taste, imagine, etc.—sometimes. There are thus central systems of some kind, but about these little is understood.

The evidence seems compelling, indeed overwhelming, that fundamental aspects of our mental and social life, including language, are determined as part of our biological endowment, not acquired by learning, still less by training, in the course of our experience. Many find this conclusion offensive. They would prefer to believe that humans are shaped by the environment, not that they develop in a manner that is predetermined in essential respects. I mentioned earlier the remarkable dominance of the behaviorist conception that language and other aspects of our beliefs and knowledge, and of our culture in general, are determined by experience. The Marxist tradition too has characteristically held that humans are products of history and society, not determined by their biological nature; of course this is not true of physical properties, such as the possession of arms rather than wings or the property of undergoing puberty at roughly a certain age, but it is held to be true of intellectual, social, and general cultural life. This standard view makes nonsense of the essentials of Marx's own thought, I believe, for reasons already briefly indicated, but let us put that aside; there is no doubt that it is proclaimed as a point of doctrine by many who call themselves Marxists. For several centuries now the dominant intellectual tradition in Anglo-American thought adopted similar conceptions. In this empiricist tradition it was held that the constructions of the mind result from a few simple operations of association on the basis of contiguity, phenomenal similarity, and so on, perhaps extended by a capacity for induction from a limited class of cases to a larger class of the same type. These resources must then suffice for all intellectual achievements, including language learning and much else.

Within this array of doctrines there are some differences, but the similarities are much more striking. One striking feature is that, although they have been widely believed, indeed asserted as virtual doctrinal truths, they are supported by no compelling evidence. In fact, attention to the simplest facts suffices to undermine them, as I have indicated throughout these lectures. If there were any truth to these doctrines, human beings would be miserable creatures indeed, extremely limited in their capacities, unlike one another, mere reflections of some accidental experience. I made the point earlier in connection with physical growth, and the same is true in the domains of intellectual, social, cultural life.

When some doctrine has such a powerful grip on the intellectual imagination over such a broad range and when it has little in the way of empirical support but is rather in conflict with the evidence at every point, it is fair to ask why the beliefs are so firmly maintained. Why should intellectuals be so wedded to the belief that humans are shaped by the environment, not determined by their nature?

In earlier years environmentalism was held to be a "progressive" doctrine. It undermined the belief that each person has a natural place fixed by nature: lord, servant, slave, and so on. It is true that if people have no endowments, then they are equal in endowments: equally miserable and unfortunate. Whatever appeal such a view may once have had, it is hard to take it seriously today. In fact, it was dubious even then; as noted, the traditional dualism to which it was opposed had deeper and far more persuasive reasons for assuming the essential unity of the human species and the lack of significant variation within it in any of these respects.

Such arguments for environmentalism are often heard today in connection with debates over race and IQ and the like. Again, it is true that if humans have no biologically determined intellectual endowments, then there will be no correlation between IQ (a socially determined property) and anything else: race, sex, or whatever. Again, though the motivation can be appreciated, it is difficult to take the argument seriously. Let us pretend for the moment that race and IQ are well-defined properties, and let us suppose that some correlation is found between them. Perhaps a person of a particular race, on the average, is likely to have a slightly higher IQ than a person of another race. Notice first that such a conclusion would have essentially null scientific interest. It is of no interest to discover a correlation between two traits selected at random, and if someone happens to be interested in this odd and pointless question, it would make far more sense to study properties that are much more clearly defined, say, length of fingernails and eye color. So the interest of the discovery must lie in the social domain. But here, it is clear that the discovery is of interest only to people who believe that each individual must be treated not as what he or she is but rather as an example of a certain category (racial, sexual, or whatever). To anyone not afflicted with these disorders, it is of zero interest whether the average value of IQ for some category of persons is such-and-such. Suppose we were to discover the height has a slight correlation with ability to do higher mathematics. Would that imply that no one under a certain height should be encouraged to study higher mathematics, or would it mean that each person should be considered as an individual, encouraged to study higher mathematics if their talents and interests so indicate? Obviously the latter, even though it would then turn out that a slightly higher percentage of taller people would end up pursuing this path. Since we do not suffer from the social disease of "heightism," the issue interests no one.

Surely people differ in their biologically determined qualities. The world would be too horrible to contemplate if they did not. But discovery of a correlation between some of these qualities is of no scientific interest and of no social significance, except to racists, sexists, and the like. Those who argue that there is a correlation between race and IQ and those who deny this claim are contributing to racism and other disorders, because what they are saying is based on the assumption that the answer to the question makes a difference; it does not, except to racists, sexist, and the like.

Case by case it is difficult to take seriously the idea that environmentalism is somehow "progressive" and should therefore be adopted as doctrine. Furthermore, the issue is irrelevant, because the question is one of truth, not doctrine. Questions of fact cannot be resolved on the basis of ideological commitment. As I have observed throughout, we should be delighted that environmentalism is utterly misconceived, but the question of truth or falsity is not resolved by our preference for one or another outcome of inquiry.

Although factual questions are not resolved by doctrines of faith, it sometimes makes sense to inquire into the relation between ideological commitments and scientific beliefs. This is particularly appropriate in a case such as the one under discussion, a case in which beliefs about matters of fact are held by the intellectual community over such a broad range, over such a long period, and with such passion and intensity, in the face of rather obvious considerations of fact and logic. Why do these environmentalist ideas have such appeal to intellectuals?

One possible answer lies in the role that intellectuals characteristically play in contemporary—and not so contemporary—society. Since intellectuals are the ones who write history, we should be cautious about the alleged "lessons of history" in this regard; it would not be surprising to discover that the version of history presented is self-serving, and indeed it is. Thus the standard image is that the intellectuals are fiercely independent, honest, defenders of the highest values, opponents of arbitrary rule and authority, and so on. The actual record reveals a different story. Quite typically, intellectuals have been ideological and social managers, serving power or seeking to assume power themselves by taking control of popular movements of which they declare themselves to be the leaders. For people committed to control and manipulation it is quite useful to believe that human beings have no intrinsic moral and intellectual nature, that they are simply objects to be shaped by state and private managers and ideologues—who, of course, perceive what is good and right. Concern for intrinsic human nature poses moral barriers in the way of manipulation and control, particularly if this nature conforms to the libertarian conceptions that I have briefly reviewed. In accordance with these conceptions, human rights are rooted in human nature, and we violate fundamental human rights when people are forced to be slaves, wage slaves, servants of external power, subjected to systems of authority and domination, manipulated and controlled "for their own good."

I rather suspect that these speculations about the otherwise quite surprising appeal of environmentalist views has more than a little truth to it.

It is sometimes argued that even if we succeed in explaining properties of human language and other human capacities in terms of an innate biological endowment, nothing has really been achieved because it remains to explain how the biological endowment developed; the problem is simply displaced, not solved. This is a curious argument. By the same logic we might argue that nothing is explained if we demonstrate that a bird does not learn to have wings but rather develops them because it is so constructed by virtue of its genetic endowment; the problem is only displaced, because it remains to explain how the genetic endowment evolved. It is perfectly correct that in each case new problems are raised. This is typically the case when we solve some problem, giving rise to others. But it would be absurd to argue that nothing has been achieved when we learn that birds grow wings by virtue of their genetic endowment, not by learning, or that humans undergo the processes of puberty because that is the way they are designed, not by observing others and deciding to do the same. True, it remains to account for the evolution of language, wings, etc. The problem is a serious one, but it belongs to a different domain of inquiry.

Can the problem be addressed today? In fact, little is known about these matters. Evolutionary theory is informative about many things, but it has little to say, as of now, about questions of this nature. The answers may well lie not so much in the theory of natural selection as in molecular biology, in the study of what kinds of physical systems can develop under the conditions of life on earth and why, ultimately because of physical principles. It surely cannot be assumed that every trait is specifically selected. In the case of such systems as language or wings it is not easy even to imagine a course of selection that might have given rise to them. A rudimentary wing, for example, is not "useful" for motion but is more of an impediment. Why then should the organ develop in the early stages of its evolution?

In some cases it seems that organs develop to serve one purpose and, when they have reached a certain form in the evolutionary process, became available for different purposes, at which point the processes of natural selection may refine them further for these purposes. It has been suggested that the development of insect wings follows this pattern. Insects have the problem of heat exchange, and rudimentary wings can serve this function. When they reach a certain size, they become less useful for this purpose but begin to be useful for flight, at which point they evolve into wings. Possibly human mental capacities have in some cases evolved in a similar way.

Take the human number faculty. Children have the capacity to acquire the number system. They can learn to count and somehow know that it is possible to continue to add one indefinitely. They can also readily acquire the technique of arithmetical calculation. If a child did not already know that it is possible to add one indefinitely, it could never learn this fact. Rather, taught the numerals 1, 2, 3, etc., up to some number n, it would assume that that is the end of the story. It seems that this capacity, like the capacity for language, lies beyond the intellectual range of otherwise intelligent apes. It was, incidentally, thought for a time that certain birds could be taught to count. Thus it was shown that some birds could be taught that if they are presented with four dots, then they can find food in the fourth container in a linear array. The task could be performed up to about seven items, leading to the conclusion that birds can count. But the conclusion is incorrect. The most elementary property of the number system is that the series of numbers goes on indefinitely; you can always add one more. Birds may have certain limited capacities to match arrays of not too many items, but that has nothing to do with the faculty of number. The ability to count is not "more of the same" but something entirely different in character.

How did the number faculty develop? It is impossible to believe that it was specifically selected. Cultures still exist today that have not made use of this faculty; their language does not contain a method for constructing indefinitely many number words, and the people of these cultures are not aware of the possibility of counting. But they certainly have the capacity. Adults can quickly learn to count and to do arithmetic if placed in the appropriate environment, and a child from such a tribe, raised in a technological society, could become an engineer or a physicist as readily as anyone else. The capacity is present but latent.

In fact, the capacity was latent and unused throughout almost all of human history. It is only recently in evolutionary terms, at a time when human evolution had reached its current stage, that the number faculty was manifested. Plainly it is not the case that people who could count, or who could solve problems of arithmetic or number theory, were able to survive to produce more offspring, so that the capacity developed through natural selection. Rather, it developed as a by-product of something else, and was available for use when circumstances called it forth.

At this point one can only speculate, but it is possible that the number faculty developed as a by-product of the language faculty. The latter has features that are quite unusual, perhaps unique in the biological world. In technical terms it has the property of "discrete infinity." To put it simply, each sentence has a fixed number of words: one, two, three, forty-seven, ninety-three, etc. And there is no limit in principle to how many words the sentence may contain. Other systems known in the animal world are quite different. Thus the system of ape calls is finite; there are a fixed number, say, forty. The so-called bee language, on the other hand, is infinite, but it is not discrete. A bee signals the distance of a flower from the hive by some form of motion; the greater the distance, the more the motion. Between any two signals there is in principle another, signaling a distance in between the first two, and this continues down to the ability to discriminate. One might argue that this system is even "richer" than human language, because it contains "more signals" in a certain mathematically well-defined sense. But this is meaningless. It is simply a different system, with an entirely different basis. To call it a "language" is simply to use a misleading metaphor.

Human language has the extremely unusual, possibly unique, property of discrete infinity, and the same is true of the human number faculty. In fact, we might think of the human number faculty as essentially an "abstraction" from human language, preserving the mechanism of discrete infinity and eliminating the other special features of language. If so, that would explain the fact that the human number faculty is available though unused in the course of human evolution.

This still leaves the question of origin of human language. Here there are some speculations, nothing more, and they do not seem persuasive. It may be that at some remote period a mutation took place that gave rise to the property of discrete infinity, perhaps for reasons that have to do with the biology of cells, to be explained in terms of properties of physical mechanisms, now unknown. Without this capacity it might have been possible to "think thoughts" of a certain restricted character, but with the capacity in place, the same conceptual apparatus would be freed for the construction of new thoughts and operations such as inference involving them, and it would be possible to express and interchange these thoughts. At that point evolutionary pressures might have shaped the further development of the capacity, at least in part. Quite possibly other aspects of its evolutionary development again reflect the operation of physical laws applying to a brain of a certain degree of complexity. We simply do not know.

This seems to me roughly where things stand today. In particular areas, such as the study of language and vision, there has been substantial progress, and more is sure to come. But many questions lie beyond our intellectual grasp for the present, and perhaps forever.

Discussions

LECTURE 1

QUESTION: If a child is raised in a rich environment, then the child will develop very differently from the child who has been neglected or who has been sent to an orphanage or something like that. What's the difference?

ANSWER: Well, let me begin with a simple case that's well understood in physiology. Let's take a cat, which has a visual system rather similar to the human visual system. Now we understand by now a good bit about the physiology or the neurology of the visual system. For example, we know that the visual system of a mammal will interpret visual stimulations in terms of straight lines, angles, motions, and three-dimensional objects. So suppose I draw something like that on the board. What you see is a slightly distorted triangle. In other words you see an ideal Euclidean object somewhat distorted. And the same is probably true for a young infant or for that matter a kitten—a kitten will presumably see these lines as a distorted triangle. And there are many more complex things than that.

These again are surprising things. You don't see that figure as exactly what it is, but you see it as a distorted version of some ideal figure that doesn't exist in nature. In nature there are no straight lines.

Now the brain of a child or a kitten performs extremely complex computations, by virtue of its very nature, which yield this kind of interpretation of the physical world. That's inside the mind, without any conscious theory.

Suppose you take a kitten and you raise it with something over the eyes which allows the light to come in but not in patterns, just diffuse light. Then what we discover is that this system of computation is destroyed. So the mature cat will literally not see objects if it has only been presented with diffuse light and not patterns.

Now this illustrates a very general fact about biology of organs. There has to be sufficiently rich environmental stimulation for the genetically determined process to develop in the manner in which it is programmed to develop.

The term for this is "triggering"; that is, the experience does not determine how the mind will work but it triggers it, it makes it work in its own largely predetermined way. It is a little like an automobile. When you turn the key in the ignition, it acts like a car, not an airplane. That is because it's built like a car. But if you don't turn the key, nothing's going to happen.

In other words what the system does depends on how it is built. But it has to have the right kind of trigger to do what it's designed to do. The visual system must be presented with patterned stimulation in order to carry out the complex operations that it is built to perform.

Now let me turn to a complex case closer to yours. Let's take a young lamb. It's known that if you take that lamb and separate it from its mother and raise it in isolation, it will not perceive depth properly. Now the mother is not teaching the lamb how to perceive depth, but there is something about the interaction between a lamb and its mother which enables the visual system to work the way it's designed to work.

Now let's take a human child which is raised in an orphanage, and let's suppose the child is given the right medical care and food and has normal experience with the physical world. Nevertheless the child may be very restricted in its abilities. In fact, the child may hear language all the time just as in its home, but yet it may not learn the language properly. And the same is true with other mental capacities such as the capacity to solve problems and to be artistically creative and so on. The point is that the mind has very rich capacities, but certain kinds of stimulating environments are necessary for these capacities to function. Now a good system of raising children puts them in a stimulating, loving environment in which their natural capacities will be able to flourish. These capacities are not being taught. They are simply being allowed to function in the way in which they are designed to develop.

What the schools actually do is often exactly the opposite. The school system is designed to teach obedience and conformity and prevent the child's natural capacities from developing. Now I think there are very good social reasons for this. That's more connected with what I'll talk about this afternoon.

QUESTION: [Unintelligible on tape.]

ANSWER: The point is correct. I emphasized biological facts, and I didn't say anything about historical and social facts. And I am going to say nothing about these elements in language acquisition. The reason is that I think they are relatively unimportant. As far as we know, the development of human mental capacity is largely determined by our inner biological nature. Now in the case of a natural capacity like language, it just happens, the way you learn to walk. In other words language is not really something you learn. Acquisition of language is something that happens to you; it's not something that you do. Learning language is something like undergoing puberty. You don't learn to do it; you don't do it because you see other people doing it; you are just designed to do it at a certain time. Now there are social factors, and others that may have an effect on this biological process. For example, nutritional level may change the time of the onset of puberty by a very large factor, perhaps 2 to 1. But the real things that are happening are primarily biologically determined. There are social factors that determine rate and timing and so forth, but overwhelmingly what is happening is that the biological process is proceeding in the way in which it is determined to proceed.

When we study natural human functions, like the development of conceptual systems, and basic ways of thinking and interpreting the physical and social world around us, then it's very much like studying puberty. If we study some other features of human life, for example, the tendency of people to enter into trade, etc., then we are certainly going to have to turn to social and historical factors which suppress certain aspects of human personality and bring forth other aspects.

For example, every social revolution has had to face the problem that in peasant society, for well-known reasons, certain traits tend to be dominant, such as the desire to be independent of interaction with other people. It is often hard to convince people in a traditional peasant society to cooperate to build a common well, for example, though everyone would benefit from it. There are other social structures—parts of modern science, for example—in which cooperative joint effort is taken for granted. Now human nature does not determine either isolation or cooperation. In fact, different historical and social circumstances allow certain aspects of human nature to appear and flourish while others are suppressed. Part of any successful social revolution is getting people to understand that part of their nature is the desire to work cooperatively and in a constructive way with others who have common interests and to work to a common end. That's a very difficult thing to achieve.

In fact, there have been now several centuries of experience relevant to one very small part of this problem, namely, cooperation in the political domain. This is a goal that the industrial democracies profess and have been trying to achieve, in theory at least, for two hundred years, without very much success. So, for example, in the US, political participation means that you can ratify decisions made by others, but you cannot play any meaningful role in forming the decision. That's what we call parliamentary democracy. But that's a very primitive form of human participation and decision-making. And even though people have the formal opportunity to take part in decision-making in the political domain, the system is designed to prevent them from doing it. What is particularly relevant in the present connection is that many people don't understand that there is something lacking. Now this means that the eighteenth-century political revolution has not yet taken place, in reality. When we think about more complex situations, such as organizing workers and production and so on, then wholly new problems arise.

Now in investigating these questions, which certainly are questions of human nature and how it develops, we are crucially going to have to turn to just what you pointed to, historical and social conditions. But when we study natural human functions, like the basic methods of thinking and the conceptual structure of language, these factors play only a marginal role, except in connection with the problem that the previous question brought up, namely, that the social environment often prevents natural human creativity and so on from developing in the normal fashion, sometimes by design.

LECTURE 4

QUESTION: The mind makes the calculation of the meaning of a sentence and words instantaneously. . . . Do you think there has to be another process of assigning specific meanings to words, and does that process take place at the same time? And I would also like to know which of the many theories of meaning that have been proposed do you find most correct?

ANSWER: Well, the first part: Do you understand the meaning of the word "instantaneously"? The answer is certainly yes. In fact, again, you can demonstrate that even the understanding of a sentence is virtually at the speed of neural transmission. It is at the speed at which the nerves can transmit signals. Now about theories of meaning—that's an interesting question. I think that none of them are very successful as yet, and, in fact, I think that many of them are pretty much on the wrong track, but I'd suggest putting that off until tomorrow. If I don't get to it tomorrow, bring that up again.

QUESTION: Prof. Chomsky, you said in one of your lectures that Marxism and materialism had blocked research on language. Could you comment further on this?

ANSWER: Well, here we have to be careful. By Marxism and materialism I mean the special form of Marxism and materialism that have developed in the West in the past century, particularly since the Bolshevik Revolution, which gave a great deal of prestige to a particular version of Marxism, namely what is sometimes called Marxism-Leninism, which is simply one very small part of the very broad Marxist tradition of eighty years ago.

Now let me say that personally I don't like to use terms like "Marxism." In my own view terms like "Marxism" belong to the history of organized religion. So, for example, in science you don't have concepts like Marxism. Every modern physicist thinks that Einstein was more or less correct but you don't have a theory of Einsteinism. The reason is that Einstein was not a god. He was a human being who had extremely brilliant and important ideas, some of which were wrong, some of which were improved by later work using his ideas. So, if Einstein were born today, he would not agree with things that he had produced in 1930.

Now, personally, I think Marx was a human being, not a god. He happened to be a human being with very important ideas and a human being who made many mistakes, which is why he kept changing his views through his life. And in the past one hundred years we have found a lot more about many other mistakes. In fact, he was a human being like many other humans with very serious personality defects. For example, he destroyed the First International because it was being taken over by working class groups that he did not like. Well, these are all reasons why we should object to Marx: both for some of his personal actions and some of his intellectual errors. But that's simply to say that Marx was a human being and not a god.

Well, if we want to appreciate the intellectual contributions of the human being called Marx (as opposed to Marxism), then we will not be Marxists, just as if we want to appreciate the intellectual contributions of Albert Einstein we will not be believers in Einsteinism. In fact, to believe in Einsteinism would be not to take Einstein seriously as a human being.

Now part of the problem of contemporary political thought in my view is that it has turned Marx into a figure of organized religion, and in fact such concepts as Marxism reflect that unfortunate fact.

The same is true when we talk about concepts like materialism. There are many forms of materialism. It's a doctrine that has taken different forms through the centuries as people have understood more about the topic. So in the sixteenth century materialism meant what happens when things bump into each other. A century after Isaac Newton, materialism included forces relating objects that were not touching. Today materialism includes particles that have no mass, and who knows what materialism will be fifty years from now. In fact, I want to come back to this topic tomorrow, so I won't pursue it now. But the point I want to make is that it is possible to answer the question only if we treat the work of Karl Marx and ideas like materialism as intellectual contributions and not as divine inspiration. Then we will ask what aspects of Marx's work are useful and what must be changed. And we will ask what form of materialism makes sense and what form doesn't make sense. Very often questions are formulated which prevent any sensible answer to them. That's very common in propaganda, ideology, politics, and one of the things that we have to learn is not to fall into that trap.

If we return now to the question, insofar as Marxism and materialism are treated as religious doctrines, there is no doubt that this hampers research into language or anything else, much as other irrational commitments do. On the other hand, if we try to extract ideas from Marx's thought that are valuable for our inquiries today, we will find very little, I think, that has any bearing at all on the study of language, so in this sense his ideas neither hamper nor facilitate this study. As for materialism, it is not a well-defined set of ideas or principles, so therefore the question cannot be answered. I'll return to some of these questions tomorrow. Perhaps we can take the matter up again then.

QUESTION: Why is teaching language to adults so difficult, when children learn language without instruction so readily?

ANSWER: Scientists don't know the answer. Something must happen to the brain about the time of puberty. Nobody knows much about this. It would not be a surprising fact. Most biological capacities have a time at which they have to operate, and they won't operate before or after that time. So, for example, every child learns to walk without being instructed. If a child breaks a leg when it's born and is in a cast until eighteeen months old and then if you take the cast off, the child will be walking fairly quickly. But if you kept the cast on until seven years old, then the child would probably never learn to walk at all. Now I'm not certain of that because I don't know if there are such cases, but it is a plausible guess. Things like that have been demonstrated in experiments with animals.

I'll give you a real case. Take a pigeon. There's a certain age—I've forgotten, maybe two weeks or so—at which a pigeon has to fly. Now if you keep the pigeon in a box so it can't move its wings until this age and then you let it out of the box, it'll fly just as well as any pigeon that's been sitting in the nest all that time. But if you keep it in that box another week or two and then you let it out of the box, it'll never be able to fly. It's very probable that language is something like that.

For the language teacher, that means that you simply cannot teach a language to an adult the way a child learns a language. That's why it's such a hard job.

QUESTION: How could you use the recent findings discussed in these lectures in the teaching of languages and translation, and how do you account for connotations and other problems which remain outside of what you have been talking about?

ANSWER: Let me make a general statement. People who are involved in some practical activity such as teaching languages, translation, or building bridges should probably keep an eye on what's happening in the sciences. But they probably shouldn't take it too seriously because the capacity to carry out practical activities without much conscious awareness of what you're doing is usually far more advanced than scientific knowledge. The history of the physical sciences is interesting in this respect. Engineers knew how to do all sorts of complicated and amazing things for hundreds of years. It wasn't until the mid-nineteenth century that physics began to catch up and to provide some understanding that was actually useful for engineers. Now physics in the nineteenth century was vastly more advanced than our understanding of languages today, and building bridges is much less complex than what is actually taking place in the teaching of languages or translating. So I think the answer to your question is, I don't think modern linguistics can tell you very much of practical utility. I think it's a good idea to pay attention to what it is doing and to see if it gives you some ideas that might enable a translator or teacher to do better, but that's really for the person involved in the practical activity to decide.

Psychology and linguistics have caused a good deal of harm by pretending to have answers to those questions and telling teachers and people who deal with children how they should behave. Often the ideas presented by the scientists are totally crazy and they may cause trouble. I could give you some examples of the harm that's been done, but I won't pursue it. Well, one example just to illustrate the kind of thing you want to keep away from.

I was once invited to Puerto Rico by people at the

university. They wanted me to talk about linguistics but also to look at the language programs in the schools. Well, in Puerto Rico everyone speaks Spanish, but they have to learn English. Now at that time every child went to school for twelve years. They were taught English five days a week for twelve years, and when they came out, they couldn't say "How are you?" In fact, I might say that the only people that a non-Spanish speaker could talk to in Puerto Rico at that time were older people who hadn't been to school. So, what was happening?

Well, my wife and I were taken to some of the schools to see what was happening, and we found that they were teaching English according to the latest scientific theories. These latest advanced scientific theories at that time said that language is a habit system, and the way you learn language is by just learning the habits. So it is kind of like catching a ball or something like that. You just keep doing it, over and over again until you get good at it. They used a system that they called pattern practice. You have a certain linguistic pattern, and you just repeat it over and over again. Well, the thing that is most obvious about these methods is that they are so boring that they put you to sleep in about three minutes. So when you go into the classroom you see that the children are looking out of the window or throwing things at the teacher or something like that. They may be paying enough attention so that they can repeat what the teacher wants them to say, but it's clear that they are going to forget it three minutes later. Well, that goes on for twelve years, five days a week, and the results are predictably close to zero.

The truth of the matter is that about 99 percent of teaching is making the students feel interested in the material. Then the other 1 percent has to do with your methods. And that's not just true of languages. It's true of every subject. We've all gone to schools and colleges, and you all know that you have taken courses in school where you have learned enough to pass the exam, and then a week later you forget what the subject was. Well, that's the problem. Learning doesn't achieve lasting results when you don't see any point to it. Learning has to come from the inside; you have to want to learn. If you want to learn, you'll learn no matter how bad the methods are.

Now a Puerto Rican child of three years old wants to learn Spanish not because the child thinks about it but because the child is a biological organism that wants to learn the language of its social environment at three years old. But a ten-year-old child in Puerto Rico sees no particular reason to learn English, and if you don't give that child any reason for learning English, they are not going to do it, no matter how good your methods are. And if you use methods which are designed to ensure that no sensible person could possibly pay attention, then there's no hope.

The proper conclusion, I think, is this: Use your common sense and use your experience and don't listen too much to the scientists, unless you find that what they say is really of practical value and of assistance in understanding the problems you face, as sometimes it truly is.

LECTURE 5

QUESTION: You have talked about language as a physical object, but of course, you are talking about abstract structures like rules and phrases and so on. And for, say, a physicist—a quantum physicist, so he's talking about physical structures—is this different? Shouldn't the physical object be explained by the principles of quantum theory? That is to say, language is a physical object. The other question is whether we could imagine a brain that has a linguistic module but not a mathematical module, or are they the same thing?

ANSWER: Let me take the second question first. It is a very good question. Remember the problem posed for biological theories, that is, Why do we have the mathematical ability, since it was never a factor in evolution? Now the answer to that must be that the mathematical ability is just a reflection of some other ability. That is, the laws of physics determine that if you have that other ability, you are going to have a mathematical ability. Now, what is that other ability? Probably language. Because in fact, if you look at the structure of mathematics it turns out that in a certain abstract sense it's abstracted from the structure of language, in the way I discussed briefly in today's lecture.

Now for some speculation about human evolution. Perhaps at some time hundreds of thousands of years ago, some small change took place, some mutation took place in the cells of prehuman organisms. And for reasons of physics which are not yet understood, that led to the representation in the mind/brain of the mechanisms of discrete infinity, the basic concept of language and also of the number system. That made it possible to think, in our sense of thinking. So now humans—or prehumans— could go beyond just reacting to stimuli and could construct complex structures out of the world of their experience, and now, the world of their imagination. Perhaps that was the origin of human language.

There is a long history of study of origin of language, asking how it arose from calls of apes and so forth. That investigation in my view is a complete waste of time, because language is based on an entirely different principle than any animal communication system. It's quite possible that human gestures . . . have evolved from animal communication systems, but not human language. It has a totally different principle.

Now let's suppose this small mutation took place, which provided the capacity to deal with discrete infinity, therefore giving us the capacity to think creatively and to speak creatively, to construct new expressions that have new meanings that someone else will understand in a very specific way, and to have new thoughts that nobody ever had before. That development would have been very useful for evolution. Biological success is defined in terms of the number of organisms. Now by that measure, humans are very successful. In fact, there are five billion of us and only, I suppose, tens of thousands of chimpanzees. The main reason for the difference probably is the development of language. This may not prove successful for very long, but that's another question. In fact, apart from insects the only animal which has proliferated to the extent of humans, I imagine, is chickens. And that's because humans raise chickens. So the point is that the development of this system would have been of great biological utility.

But now once this system was developed, mathematics was there implicitly. All that was necessary was for the right stage of historical and cultural development to take place for humans to begin to realize that they had this capacity which they never had used before.

Now this is speculation, but it's fairly plausible speculation, I think. And if it's correct, then the answer to your question is that there couldn't be a mathematical capacity without a language capacity.

Now let me make one comment about the history of mathematics. If you think about the history of mathematics, say from Euclid to fairly recently, there are really two basic ideas. One idea is numbers; the other idea is the structure of three-dimensional visual space, which is based on the concept of continuity. Most of modern mathematics really develops from those two ideas. Now probably the exploration of the intuition of physical space is possible because of the nature of our visual systems, and we can have the relevant thoughts about geometrical space because we have language. A cat can't develop calculus. The other notion, of number, probably comes from our language capacity directly. That may be the explanation why the history of mathematics took the very special course that it did.

Let's turn now to the first question. In what sense is language a physical structure? We do not know for certain, but we believe that there are physical structures of the brain which are the basis for the computations and the representations that we describe in an abstract way. This relationship between unknown physical mechanisms and abstract properties is very common in the history of science. So, for example, in the nineteenth century chemists constructed abstract diagrams that were supposed to represent a complex molecule with carbon and hydrogen and oxygen attached in some fashion. But that's a completely abstract representation. For example, the chemist couldn't say what the particular parts of the diagram referred to in the physical world. In fact, it wasn't clear whether there were things corresponding to the parts of the diagram. Even now that we know better what carbon is, we recognize that it is something abstract. So, you can't hit carbon. In fact, it's a very abstract concept. But the point is that the chemists' descriptions were part of an explanatory theory. They were part of a theory from which you could predict what would happen if you sent an electric current through some physical object, for example.

Now those theories of the chemist are similar to a linguist's theory of computations of the brain. In each case the abstract theories pose a further question for the physical scientist. The question is, find the physical mechanisms that have these properties. In the early part of the twentieth century, physicists began to discover the physical entities that had the properties that had been described by the chemists. In fact, until the early part of the twentieth century, many scientists weren't convinced that there were even such things as molecules. They thought this was just an abstract idea, an abstract computational idea. In the early part of the twentieth century, evidence accumulated showing that there really are things that have these properties.

Now physics could not have developed the structure of the atom and the molecule if nineteenth-century chemistry hadn't provided the abstract theories. That's what told the physicists what they should look for. They had to look for things which had the very complicated properties described in the abstract theories. And the brain sciences are in the same state today. They have to ask the linguist or the psychologist what are the abstract structures that humans possess for which we have to search for the physical basis.

Why don't they make much progress in answering the question? The reason is partly ethical, namely, we are not allowed to do experiments on human beings. We allow ourselves to torture cats and monkeys, but, except for the police force, we don't allow ourselves to torture humans. So that means that the kinds of experiments that could give the answer are not permissible. If we had, say, Nazi doctors, they could begin to cut apart the human brain, and they could probably discover what the physical mechanisms are.

In fact, this has happened in the case of the visual system. In the last twenty-five years there have been the beginnings of an understanding of the computational processes of the visual system. Actual physical, biological systems have been identified. The work is done with cats and monkeys. Now cats and monkeys have a visual system very much like ours. So we can guess that what we're discovering about cats and monkeys is probably quite similar to what is true of humans.

But there is no other organism that has a language faculty. And, in fact, if there were such an organism, we would probably consider it human, and we would probably apply our ethical standards to it.

So, the fact is that, fortunately, the direct methods of physical investigation are closed. Part of the intellectual excitement of this field is that you cannot carry out the direct experiments and therefore you have to be much more clever about how you proceed to try to find the answers.

Let me give one final analogy: Imagine a physicist who's trying to figure out what's happening on the inside of the sun. Now the easy way to answer it would be to put a laboratory inside the sun and to do experiments. But you can't do that or the laboratory will turn into a gas. So therefore what you have to do is look at the light that reaches you from the sun. You have to try to imagine what is happening on the inside of the sun that is producing that kind of light. That's very much like trying to figure out what's going on in the physical mechanisms of the brain.

Since this is the final day and since we've had much too little time for discussion, we have asked that to save time, you submit questions in writing, and a great many of you have done so. Well, I can already see that some of these questions are very interesting but too complicated to deal with in the brief time available. I think I will have to put them aside and keep to the simpler and more pointed ones. Here is one.

QUESTION: A child can learn two languages simultaneously, one in the house and the other in the street. Does this mean that the child relates the position of the switches to the environment?

ANSWER: Well, this is a very important question which I have been pretending all along does not arise. The question is a very mysterious one. I should say the example that is raised in the question is a very striking one, because the child learns different languages, say Spanish at home and English in the streets. But, in fact, the problem is really more general, because every human being speaks a variety of languages. We sometimes call them different styles or different dialects, but they are really different languages, and somehow we know when to use them, one in one place and another in another place. Now each of these different languages involves a different switch setting. In the case of Spanish/English it is a rather dramatically different switch setting, more so than in the case of the different styles of Spanish that each of you has mastered.

Now it is a known fact that a child can learn several languages perfectly without any attention at all, which means that somehow the brain must have simultaneously several different switch settings. Now it appears that this is possible only when somehow the child associates each language with a certain kind of situation. So the child knows that this is the way you talk to your friends, and this is the way you talk to your grandmother, and so on. But, for example, if the child's parents are speaking several different languages around the dinner table, the chances are that the child is going to be extremely confused.

Somehow, young children have a theory of society and a theory of language, and they are able to link them up in some fashion to indicate that you speak this language in this social situation.

I should say that young children seem to be unaware that they are speaking different languages. There is a close friend and colleague of mine at MIT who grew up in Eastern Europe speaking five languages, and he remembers very clearly the sudden revelation that he was speaking different languages. Prior to that he had no awareness of it at all. How all this works nobody knows. It is a very interesting problem.

QUESTION: Do the similarities that you suppose exist in the languages of the world arise from a common origin?

ANSWER: Well, it is possible, but it is by no means certain. It is really a question of how human evolution took place. It is entirely possible that there was a common human origin, but the development of language took place after it split into several strains, and the language system developed in exactly the same way because of facts about biology and physics. We just do not know enough about human evolution to be able to answer this question. There are many possible answers.

QUESTION: As you seemed to reject Marxism and materialism, I wonder if you also reject investigation which involves historical and dialectical materialism? If so, what is your method of investigation?

ANSWER: Well, first of all I don't reject Marxism and materialism. Rather, I think that these terms do not mean very much. For example, I am convinced that, if Marx were alive today, he would reject a good deal of the corpus of work that we call Marxism. That would simply be because he was an intelligent human being, just as if some nineteenth-century physicist were to be reborn today, he would reject much of his own work in the nineteenth century. On the other hand, there are major elements of what we call Marxism and what we call materialism which are just part of the common intellectual background of reasonable people trying to understand the world. This includes certain elements of so-called historical materialism.

Now, as for dialectical materialism, in my view this is a rather obscure notion. I do not believe that the concept of dialectical materialism even appears in Marx's work. My recollection is that this was a phrase used only by Engels. It is clear that people do use the word "dialectical" as if they understand it, but I personally have never understood it. In fact, my own feeling is that it is a kind of ritual term which people use when they are talking about situations of conflict and so on. Personally, I do not find it a very useful idea. If other people find it useful, then fine, use it.

As for my own methods of investigation, I do not really have any. The only method of investigation is to look hard at a serious problem and try to get some ideas as to what might be the explanation for it, meanwhile keeping an open mind about all sorts of other possibilities. Well, that is not a method. It is just being reasonable, and so far as I know, that is the only way to deal with any problem, whether it is a problem in your work as a quantum physicist or whatever.

There are certain fields like psychology where people do carry out extensive study of methods of investigation. There are other fields like physics where you do not study methods of investigation. So at MIT the physics department does not have a course in experimental methods, but many psychology departments spend a lot of time on what they call methodology. Well, there is a lesson there, but I won't draw it.

QUESTION: When it comes to the meaning of words, we realize that although we use words quite precisely, it is very difficult to define or specify or determine the meaning of even simple words.

ANSWER: There are other parts of the question, but let me begin with this one. The statement is certainly correct. In fact, try to define a word like "table" or "book" or whatever, and you'll find it's extremely difficult. There is, in fact—just to give one example—a recent issue of a linguistics journal that has a long detailed article trying to give the meaning of the word "climb." And it is very complicated. But every child learns it perfectly right away.

Now that can only mean one thing. Namely, human nature gives us the concept "climb" for free. That is, the concept "climb" is just part of the way in which we are able to interpret experience available to us before we even have the experience. That is probably true for most concepts that have words for them in language. This is the way we learn language. We simply learn the label that goes with the preexisting concept. So in other words, it is as if the child, prior to any experience, has a long list of concepts like "climb," and then the child is looking at the world to figure out which sound goes with the concept. We know that the child figures it out with only a very small number of presentations of the sound.

Well, that leads to the second part of the question: What do you think about different theories of meaning? There are no very good theories of meaning. In fact, the more advanced parts of the theory of meaning, in my opinion, have to do with what I have been talking about for the last five days. Remember that every single example that I have given was part of the theory of meaning. So, I was trying to figure out why certain sentences mean certain things and not other things. In fact, most of the theory of meaning is called syntax. It is a theory of representations in the mind—mental representations and the computational systems that form and modify these representations. That is the major part of the theory of meaning. In addition, there are other parts, for example, asking why the words *seguir* ("follow") and *perseguir* ("pursue") are related as they are, that is, with some relation involving the notion of human intention. So the word *perseguir* expresses an intention to follow, but *seguir* has no assumption about any intention at all. Well, that is an interesting aspect of the theory of meaning. It leads us to the search for the components that enter into the meanings of words, components like intention or goal and so on. There is a lot to say about these concepts. They show up in normal spoken language in a very interesting fashion and also show up in a very similar fashion in what is called sign language, that is, the language that uses physical motion that has been devised by deaf people, but that uses motions and the form of the hand instead of spoken words. This has very much the structure of natural spoken language, and almost certainly is based upon the same language module. These systems also use concepts like intention and goal and so on.

There is a good deal more to the theory of meaning, for example, questions about the relation of meaning to use and to verification, questions about the way words come to refer to things, and so on. These are the topics that constitute most of the content of what is usually called the theory of meaning. But about these topics I think there is very little to say of a constructive nature.

QUESTION: Is language the first system of signs acquired by the child?

ANSWER: Well, that's more or less a question of definition. For example, the child learns to point before it speaks. You could think of pointing as a kind of sign system, but that's really more or less a question of definition, not a factual question. Incidentally, there is some recent work on apes which suggests that apes may not be capable of pointing, which if true, would be quite interesting. Children do it again without any instruction. In fact, children can even figure out what an adult is looking at. For example, if I am looking at that pitcher of water over there and there is a young infant observing, the infant can somehow figure out that I am looking at that thing. That is quite an incredible feat. It seems that apes can't do it. That may be part of the reason why children can learn language. You can imagine how hard it would be for people to learn language if they didn't know what speakers were looking at when they talked. Well, one could think of all these things as prelinguistic sign systems.

QUESTION: Is it easier and quicker for a child to acquire language than other systems of signs?

ANSWER: Well, there's no simple answer, some yes and some no—for example, pointing yes, cubist art no. In fact, there are all sorts of different answers for different systems.

QUESTION: Is there an innate component for each language?

ANSWER: Well, presumably not. That is, it seems there is just one language faculty, and it can handle any human language.

QUESTION: Is there a close relation between science and production? For example, does Descartes's thought coincide with a certain level of productive development?

ANSWER: Well, that's an interesting question. There are some simple answers. For example, Cartesian thought was very much influenced by the automata of the seventeenth century. The achievements of seventeenth-century science and technology certainly suggested many of the themes of Cartesian thought, and there's no doubt at all that contemporary electronic computers have stimulated scientific thought in a number of directions.

Now I know that the questioner did not have that kind of thing in mind. The question is, Are there some deeper and more subtle connections between the level of production and the kind of thinking that can be done? My suspicion is that the answer to that is no. So I don't think there would be very much difficulty in teaching modern physics or modern mathematics to a person who knows only Stone Age technology. It would be difficult in the sense that certain experiments and practical applications would not be available, but I'm not convinced that anything deeper than that would be involved.

. . .

There's an interesting question by a mathematician about formal classification of languages, but since he's the only person in the audience who is going to understand the answer, I think I'll skip it. Maybe if there's a minute later—whoever it was—we could talk about it.

QUESTION: Have there been some changes in the theory since the publication of the Pisa lectures (that was about 1980), and what are they and what articles, books, and so on?

ANSWER: Yes, there have been a lot of changes. In fact, I brought along with me to Nicaragua a book that just appeared which reviews some of these changes. It's here in the library. Some of it is general discussion, very much of the kind I've been giving here, and parts of it go into much more technical work. In fact, that was written about a year and a half ago and by now there are all sorts of new things. It happens to be a very exciting moment in the field, and things are happening every day. To answer the question properly would take another five lectures, at least.

QUESTION: What is the relationship between linguistics and politics? Victory for the US in Vietnam and victory for the generative theory in linguistics?

ANSWER: Well, remember, what I said is that the US attained a partial victory in Vietnam. There was also a partial defeat in Indochina. In other words, Indochina is independent; it's not a US colony. At home there was a huge defeat for the US government. That's a very important fact, which I'll talk about this afternoon. However, in my view none of this has anything to do with the relation between linguistics and politics. These relations, if they exist, are conceptual and abstract.

I more or less had that in mind in the earlier discussion, but I didn't quite get to discuss it, so let me add a few sentences to bring the topics together. A crucial part of language is the creative aspect of language use and the elements of human nature which make it essential to our intellectual lives. Now that is a conclusion of science, we have good evidence about that. In the realm of social thought we don't really have good evidence for anything, so our conceptions are more an expression of our hopes and our intuitive judgments and our personal experience and the ways we understand history than they are the product of any substantial scientific understanding. My own personal commitments and hopes are more or less of the sort that I described; that is, they are based on the ideas of libertarian socialism, that is, rooted in some of the ideas of Rousseau, Humboldt, Marx, Bakunin, and others, with a crucial concern for the opportunity for meaningful creative work under the control of the worker. Here I would understand work in a very broad sense, and in fact, I would consider that these ideas extend to control over every other aspect of social and personal life.

Well, do these two concepts have anything to do with one another? They may. It could be that there's a connection between the creative aspect of language use, which is part of the human essence, part of what Marx called the species character of the human being (the character of the species); there may be a connection between that and the idea of a distinctively human need for productive and creative work (including intellectual work) under one's own control, that is, control of producers over production, which is the essence of Marxist thought, among other intellectual traditions. So there may be a connection between these two things. They're conceptually rather similar, and that connection, if it holds, if it is real, which it may well be, is independent of victories and defeats in imperialist wars.

QUESTION: How can you distinguish language from thought when we know that deaf people (or people whose language has been affected in some way) cannot develop the different thinking processes. What I mean is that there is a tight relation between problems of language and the development of thinking processes.

ANSWER: First of all, let's be careful about deaf people. If deaf people have developed sign language, then there are no intellectual defects at all. Many people who are not deaf think that deaf people have deficits because we just don't understand their language.

But properly understood, what you say is quite true. If a person doesn't have any languages at all, then there will undoubtedly be severe intellectual deficits, and this has nothing to do with deafness. There are some known cases of children who have been brought up in isolation, for example, by sadistic parents. In fact, there is one well-studied case of a girl who was kept in a room never hearing a word of language until she was, I think, thirteen years old. Her intellectual deficits were enormous, though it's also interesting to see how much she was able to do.

Now, I don't think that any of this tells us much about the relationship between language and thought. The fact is that if you have not developed language, you simply don't have access to most of human experience, and if you don't have access to experience, then you're not going to be able to think properly. But that's a little bit like the fact that if a person is brought up in a device which didn't allow him to move his arms or legs, then at age thirteen such a person would never be able to learn how to walk or to pick up something or whatever. As I mentioned, we know from experimental work on animals that the parts of the brain that are concerned with perception simply do not develop properly, in fact, they degenerate severely, unless they are presented with the right kind of stimulation at the right period of development. Well, all of this again just tells us that any organism needs a rich and stimulating environment in order for its natural capacities to emerge. Again, to go back to the image of teaching being like allowing a flower to grow well, if you don't give the flower water it's not going to grow to be a flower. It's not learning from the water to be a flower—if it was a tree, it would use the same water to grow to be a tree. I think much of the same kind of thing happens in human development, including the development of language and thought.

Index

203 Mathematical ability. *See*
Number faculty
Mathematics, history of, 184–
185
Maze running, 147–148
Meaning
innate concepts and, 30–34,
134, 190–192
instantaneous calculation of,
176
theories of, 191–192
of words, 28–30
Mechanical principles, human
behavior and, 138–141
Mentalism, 8
Mentalistic terminology, 145
Mental representation
empty categories in, 75, 81,
84, 90–92, 99
logical structure and, 89–90
Methodology, 189–190
Mind-body problem, 138–147
Mind/brain. *See also* Cognitive
system
properties of, 15, 17
universal grammar and, 73–
74
Miskito, 69–70
Modularity, 161
Moral judgment, 152–154

Natural selection, species
capacities and, 167–169.
See also Evolution
Newton, Isaac, 143, 178
Nominative case, 102
nos, 96–98, 130
Noun phrase (NP), 68–69
Nouns, case assignment and,
112
NP. *See* Noun phrase
Null subject. *See pro*
Null subject parameter, 63–
65, 67, 119–120
Number agreement, 128

Number faculty, 167–169,
181–185

Oblique case, 102, 112
Operators
case theory and, 113–114
variable binding and, 87–89,
96
Order. *See* Word order

Parameters
acquisition and, 62–63, 70,
134, 188
language differences and,
63–65, 67–68, 100, 133–
134
language properties and, 16–
17, 19
parecer, 107–109, 116
complement of, 115
semantic role assignment
and, 131
vs. *seems,* 107–110
Passive construction, 119–120
Pathology, language and, 38–39
pedir, 127–128
Peirce, Charles Sanders, 158
Perception problem, 4
persuadir, 31–34
Philosophy
linguistics and, 6
science and, 2–3
Phonetic distinctions, 72. *See
also* Sound structure
Phrase structure, 68–69, 110–
112
Physics
abstract concepts in, 7, 185–
186
explanation in, 144–146
Plato's problem, 3–4, 134
analogy and, 20–21, 24, 26
language faculty and, 17,
24–27, 131
structure dependence and,
44–47